THE
OPEN-BOOK
EXPERIENCE

Also by John Case

*Open-Book Management: The Coming
Business Revolution*

*From the Ground Up: The Resurgence
of American Entrepreneurship*

Digital Future

Understanding Inflation

THE
OPEN-BOOK
EXPERIENCE

Lessons from Over 100 Companies

Who Successfully

Transformed Themselves

JOHN CASE

PERSEUS BOOKS

Reading, Massachusetts

ISBN 0-7382-0040-9

Library of Congress Catalog Card Number: 98-88745

Perseus Books is a member of the Perseus Books Group

Cover design by Andrew Newman
Text design by Joyce Weston
Set in 11-point Sabon by Rob Mauhar, CIP of Coronado

1 2 3 4 5 6 7 8 9—0201009998
First paperback printing, December 1998

Perseus Books are available at special discounts for bulk purchases in the U.S. by corporations, institutions, and other organizations. For more information, please contact the Special Markets Department at HarperCollins Publishers, 10 East 53rd Street, New York, NY 10022, or call 212-207-7528.

Find us on the World Wide Web at
http://www.aw.com/gb/

To the men and women
who are creating open-book companies

Contents

Games: Open-Book Management in Microcosm

Implementing Open-Book Management

A Revolution in Progress

This book can help you transform your company. It can help you make it more profitable, more competitive, and a better place to work.

I make this statement with such confidence for a reason, and it isn't that I'm so smart.

Here's the story. For the last four years, my associates and I have been studying a truly extraordinary group of companies—companies that are literally inventing a new way of running a business. These companies range in size from tiny, family-run shops to divisions of some of the world's largest corporations. They are all over the economic map: in manufacturing, business services, energy production, transportation, publishing, high tech, health care, the retail and distribution industries, hospitality, professional services, even a few nonprofits. As I write, we have gathered detailed information on more than 100, and we learn of others every day (too many to keep up with!). Most of them, so far, are in the United States and Canada. But we've heard of similar businesses in countries as remote from one another as Australia, Brazil, and the United Kingdom.

The approach these companies are developing has come to be known as *open-book management*. If you read this book, you'll learn open-book management straight from the people who are doing it. You'll see how it works, why it strengthens a company, how and why it boosts business performance.

In some ways—and I'd better admit this right away since I'm the one who originally coined the phrase—the term *open-book management* doesn't do the new approach justice.

Yes, open-book companies do share full financial information with their employees. They share not just companywide income statements and balance sheets but business-unit P&Ls, budgets, forecasts, and all the other critical data that senior managers have traditionally kept locked up in their offices (or in their heads). So the open-book moniker makes at least some sense. But open-book management isn't a set of techniques for disseminating information; it's a systematic approach to running a business, and it involves far-reaching changes in how a company operates. Adopt the open-book approach and you'll find yourself doing planning and budgeting in a new way. You'll have a whole new view of how to use financial reports. You'll find that you have to provide new kinds of training for your employees and probably revamp your compensation system as well. Open-book management is anything but a quick fix. It's a way of doing business, and thinking about business, that reshapes an entire organization.

But open-book management pays off in ways no quick fix ever can. It changes how people think and act every day on the job. It creates an organization in which everyone understands, cares about, and works to further the company's business objectives. The people in conventional companies, however well paid they may be, typically view themselves as hired hands. Their task is to do whatever is in their job description—or whatever the boss tells them to do. People in open-book companies have a different view; they see themselves as businesspeople. Whatever their job description, their real task is to help the company succeed. Ultimately, it's that new definition of work and job responsibilities that makes the difference.

My last book was called *Open-Book Management: The Coming Business Revolution*. It told the story of this phenomenon as it was emerging. This book is different. The last few years have added enormous amounts to our understanding of open-book management. The approach has been adopted by many more companies, of many different sizes, operating in many more industries. Not surprisingly, it has evolved. Managers and business owners have learned how to apply the basic ideas in a wide variety of contexts. They have developed dozens of useful implementation tools. The revolution that was coming then is in progress now.

This book reviews the principles of open-book management, so there's no need to go back and read the previous one if you missed it. But then it picks up where the last book left off. It explains open-book management as a system. It describes the implementation process in detail. Mainly, it provides a compendium of tools and techniques—tools and techniques that have been developed and tested in the real world and that you can adapt or borrow for your own company. The Resources page at the back of this book tells you how to get additional information, including information about getting in touch with other open-book companies.

If you're already an open-book partisan, you can skip the introduction and the first chapter. If you're skeptical, though—and particularly if you wonder who really needs yet another book about yet another method of reshaping business—please start on the next page and plow right on through. The introduction lays to rest (I hope) the idea that just because we have been through Excellence and TQM and reengineering and all the other buzzwords of the last 15 years, we can somehow quit thinking about how businesses are managed. The first chapter explains what open-book management is and illustrates a few of the many, many ways in which it can transform a company.

From then on it's all how-to. When you finish this book, you should know what open-book management is all about, how it's implemented, and what it looks like in practice. And you should have a pretty good idea of how it might work in your own business. Right there, of course—in the envisioning of an alternative— is where the transformation of any company has to start.

Do We *Really* Need Another New Approach to Management?

W e do. We have been putting Band-Aids on the old one for long enough. Just look at the central business challenge that faces companies today and at all the tools they have frantically been hauling out to meet it. Then consider the problems that remain.

The challenge itself is simple: boosting performance. What matters in today's economy is whether you deliver value to the customer and whether the value you deliver this year is better than the value you delivered last year. If it isn't, it's a safe bet that some other company's will be. Before long, that other company might as well have its hand in your company's picnic basket, for it will be eating your lunch.

Performance didn't used to be so important. Up until 1980 or so it was enough for a company to be the biggest in its marketplace, or the oldest, or the best known. It was enough to have a good location, a decent product or service, a reasonable price. Cozy regulatory arrangements protected some industries. Others were dominated by three or four giant corporations that limited their competition to jostling for a point or two of market share. That now-distant time was the era of three TV networks (and no cable), a few big automobile manufacturers and computer makers, one or two locally owned newspapers and hospitals per city, a mom-and-pop drugstore in every neighborhood, and One Big Phone Company. Like elected officials, the incumbents in a market had a huge advantage. Businesses could count on operating today about the way they did yesterday.

Then came the deluge.

One big change was deregulation: industries from telecommunications to trucking were opened up to competition, and the competition proved fierce. A second was the globalization of the marketplace: suddenly some of the biggest and most powerful U.S. companies came under attack from foreign competitors. Meanwhile, revolutionary new computer and communications technologies were creating whole new industries and reshaping others. Savvy entrepreneurs began building companies that did things old-line businesses had thought impossible. (Overnight delivery anywhere in the United States? Are you nuts?) The effect of all these changes was to ratchet up the performance bar, and hence to undercut the old sources of competitive advantage. Suddenly it wasn't necessarily an asset to be the biggest guy on the block or to have well-established distribution channels. It might even be a liability. In the new economy, what mattered was the ability to move fast and to deliver value right now. What mattered was performance.

The history of management (and management fads) in recent years is a history of companies' attempts to boost their performance. If you were listening closely, you could hear three different battle cries.

Redraw the corporate boundaries! If you're cynical by nature, you'd call this the investment-banker solution. Companies merged. They acquired. They divested. They reorganized and restructured themselves. Weirdly, this battle cry sometimes meant "We gotta get bigger" and sometimes meant "We gotta get smaller." Banks, telecommunications and media companies, and health-care chains all sought size. They merged with erstwhile competitors or simply bought them out, creating ever-larger businesses. Manufacturers took the opposite tack. They shut down plants, sold off divisions, and cut product lines. Measured by number of employees, the average manufacturing company is smaller now than it used to be.

We have to change the way we do things! This is the cry that kept the systems consultants in business. Companies hired consultants to bring in new computer networks, to teach them new quality procedures, to redesign all sorts of processes. They learned TQM, just-in-time, *kaizen*, zero defects, the Five Whys, lean thinking. And they reengineered. (Boy, did they reengineer.) They slashed order-processing time from hours to minutes. They boosted throughput by factors of two and three and four. Or at least the successful ones did. Sometimes, as even its proponents admitted, reengineering efforts flopped. But when one consultant was given the bum's rush, another was waiting at the door.

We have to get our people on board! Here's where the human-resources folks came to the fore. Companies sought to *motivate* and *educate* their employees. They wanted to *inspire* and *empower* them. So they set up training programs, quality classes, and retreats (preferably with ropes courses or white-water rafting). They instituted suggestion systems, performance-appraisal systems, new compensation plans. They put employees on teams—work teams, self-managing teams, customer-service teams, cross-functional teams, problem-solving teams. They tried to create corporate cultures that imbued employees with that elusive one-big-happy-family feeling.

The typical big company, of course, did *all* these things, year after year, sometimes all at once. This strategy wasn't always productive. It was hard for employees to feel all warm and fuzzy about those new teams, for example, when the execs in the corner offices were announcing the downsizing plans. It was also hard for anybody, employee or manager, to get too excited about this year's initiative when last year's had disappeared without a trace. A plant I visited had instituted a zero-defects program a couple of years earlier. When I asked about it, the manager rolled his eyes. "Yeah, we all wore those ZD buttons for a year. And for what?"

At any rate, the real problems were more fundamental.

The restructurings essentially treated people as if they were disposable. When "Chainsaw Al" Dunlap lopped off half the workforce of Sunbeam Corporation, thousands of people ended up out on the street. It was a scene repeated at AT&T, Digital Equipment Corporation, and a hundred other big companies. But even in less brutal cases—in mergers, for example—employees found themselves fighting desperately to hold on to their jobs. Reengineerings and other process fixes could be devastating, too. So many reengineering efforts led to so many pink slips that the word itself became a virtual synonym for layoff.

The human-resources initiatives didn't treat people as if they were disposable; rather, they treated them as if they were lab rats. They taught employees to better their performance in this corner or that corner of the business, quality one year and team-building the next and customer service the year after that. They never taught people how all those things fit together, or what management was thinking (*if* it was thinking) when it launched the initiative. Nor did they give employees a reason to care. People trundled off to training programs, joined their teams, endured the new performance-review systems—and never learned what those new skills had to do with the company's business needs or why they should give a hoot in hell about those business needs anyway.

So the legacy of the last fifteen years, after a decade and a half of managerial attempts to boost companies' performance, is decidedly mixed.

On the one hand, there's no doubt that most businesses are performing better than they used to. Quality is higher, service is better, costs have been slashed again and again. This should come as no surprise. The marketplace really is more competitive these days, and companies that failed to adapt are no longer with us. Then, too, technology is changing at a pace that we haven't seen in a century. Companies have to change how they do things just to take advantage of the new technology.

On the other hand, the *people* in companies aren't doing so well. They are anxious and frustrated. They regard their employers with a baleful mixture of mistrust and misgiving. Above all, they are deeply cynical. "The frontline workforce is not sprinkled with a handful of cynics," wrote T. J. Larkin and Sandar Larkin in *Harvard Business Review*, "it is cynical through and through."* The icon of our age isn't the Organization Man, it's Dilbert and his pals.

Does this matter? It does, and not only because it would be nice to have an economy in which people felt good about the work they do and the organizations they work for. It matters because, ultimately, a business's performance depends on its people.

Corporate reorganizations, after all, are self-limiting. You can't keep merging and acquiring forever. Reengineering your processes is also self-limiting. Once you have eliminated most of your quality problems, most of your downtime and bottlenecks and inefficiencies, you reach a point of diminishing returns. Moreover, what you find is that your competitors have done everything you did. Your performance may be as good as theirs. But it isn't any better.

---

*"Reaching and Changing Frontline Employees," *Harvard Business Review*, May–June 1996, p. 96.

Really the *only* way for a company to boost performance consistently over the long term is to have employees who work enthusiastically and effectively and who take responsibility for their own work. Good systems—meaning good procedures and equipment—are indispensable. But what makes the difference in the end is whether the employees doing the job *think* about doing it just a little better and *care* whether they do or don't.

No book of procedures can make somebody who's dealing with a customer do so with a genuine smile and a desire to help. No quality-assurance system can guarantee that manufacturing workers catch that almost-perfect part and pull it before it's shipped, or figure out how to solve a bottleneck before it even arises so that a customer's order can go out on time and still be free of defects. No amount of reengineering can make an employee want to go the extra mile, to beat (not just meet) the schedule or the budget, to come up with an idea for a new product or a new way to deliver a service.

That human dimension of business—the wanting, the caring, the enthusiasm, the problem solving and initiative taking—is where more and more competitive battles are being won or lost. But to get to a point where people do care, we need a new approach to management, an approach that doesn't merely try to patch over the flaws of the old one, but that starts from scratch, with a new set of assumptions about how people in an organization work together.

CHAPTER ONE

Transforming a Company through Open-Book Management

Open-book management starts with an assumption about how people in a company work best together. It then creates a system that allows people to work in just that way. That's really all there is to it.

The assumption is this: *a company performs best when its people see themselves as partners in the business,* rather than as hired hands—when they concern themselves not just with doing their jobs, but with the business objectives of the company.

Now this is an assumption with a rather short pedigree. Frederick W. Taylor, the father of scientific management, would have thought it absurd. He believed that people in the lower ranks—meaning everybody other than a few executives and planners—should do as they were told, period. Moreover, they would be told precisely what to do and how to do it. *That* assumption was enshrined in managerial thinking (and written into union agreements) for a century. Whether by contract or by custom, the job description and the accompanying work rules and procedures came to be sacrosanct. Over the years, the phrase "Hey, that's not *my* job" must have issued from a million lips.

Taylor's ideas haven't been altered much even in recent years. All those initiatives that teach employees to monitor their own quality, for example, or to work in teams are still telling employees what to do; they're just telling them to do things differently. And look closely at all those reengineerings of work flow. Employees usually wind up with more to do (and more to worry about) after a work redesign, but the job is still their *job.* It's still management that looks at the big picture, sees the company's needs, and issues the marching orders. And it's still an employee's job to follow those orders.

Here and there, to be sure, the idea that employees should learn to think like owners has been creeping into companies' internal dialogues about how they can boost their performance.

Profit-based bonuses, for example, are no longer confined to top executives, but are being distributed through the ranks in more and more companies. The hope is that employees will begin caring whether the company is making money and will act accordingly. It's the same with stock options, which also are being distributed much more widely than they used to be. Sanford I. Weill, CEO of Travelers Group, could have been speaking for a number of likeminded businesspeople when he explained the rationale behind his company's broad-based stock-option plan. The idea, said Weill, is to get everyone "to think like owners and build our wealth."* The several thousand companies with employee stock ownership plans (ESOPs) also say they want their employees to think and act like the owners they are. United Airlines, for one, has conducted a series of elaborate (and expensive) training exercises to build an "ownership culture."

But though the idea here is noble, the practice so far has been weak. Big companies such as United have to overcome decades of labor-management animosity and have as yet made only a small dent. Even in less rancorous situations, a few shares of stock in a retirement plan—or a bonus paid according to a profitability formula that no one really understands—may or may not induce an employee to care how the company performs. But even if it does, so what? There's a world of difference between thinking like an owner and knowing how to act like one. Workers may *want* the business to succeed but may have no idea how to help it do so.

If you really want employees to think and act like owners—if you want them to see themselves as partners in the business and to know how to help it perform better—you have to organize your company according to three principles. Taken together, these principles are the building blocks of an open-book system.

First, you have to create a *transparent* company, a company in which everyone, not just those at the top, sees and understands the real numbers.

Business Week, July 22, 1996, p. 81c.

What are the real numbers? They're the numbers that management uses to run the business and to gauge its performance. Some of them are operational measures, such as units shipped, customers served, and share of the market. Many are financial figures: gross margin, income before tax, return on assets. The real numbers include the income statement, balance sheet, and cash-flow statement that most businesses prepare at the end of every month or quarter. They also include all the numbers that will ultimately have an impact on those financials: business objectives; operational targets; budgets; forecasts; year-to-date performance, month-to-date performance, actual compared to plan. These data are a company's guidance system. They shape management's actions. They allow employees to gauge the success of what they do. When everybody sees the same information, everybody knows what's working and what isn't.

Second, you need a system of *joint accountability*, a system that holds everybody responsible for his or her part in the company's performance.

Executives and senior managers—but not many lower-level employees, at least in most companies—understand that a business unit's performance reflects a hundred different elements: sales, costs, customer satisfaction, labor productivity, budget variances, R&D expenditures, and so on. Managers who are responsible for these numbers learn to identify and watch the variables that drive them. They learn to forecast and reforecast, to analyze the budget for possible trade-offs and fallbacks, to figure out ways by which they can get more or better work done in the same amount of time. In open-book companies, employees, too, begin learning all these skills. They have to, because they, not just their bosses, are suddenly responsible for making their numbers.

Third, you give people a *stake in success* as well as pay them for their time.

Employees work for a wage. Owners share in the profits, and ultimately in the wealth, that their companies create. If you want people to think and act like owners, you have to pay them accordingly. So open-book management necessarily involves a healthy bonus plan. It works best when employees own stock as well.

Unlike conventional bonuses, open-book bonuses are always tied to some easily understood measure or measures of business-unit performance, and progress toward the goal is tracked publicly.

The system is thus wholly transparent. People see and understand the numbers that determine success. They learn to take responsibility for their part in making those numbers. They know beforehand how they will be rewarded if their unit achieves its goals.

Implementing these principles—creating an open-book company—is both harder and easier than implementing any other managerial idea that has come down the pike in recent years.

On the hard side: it is an ongoing practice—a system, not a program. You can't implement only part of it, or at least you can't expect to accomplish much if you do. If you want to turn your business into an open-book company, you'll have to proceed on a dozen different fronts. It's time-consuming and sometimes frustrating, as the managers whose words you'll read in this book would be the first to admit. Hiring a quality consultant is one helluva lot easier.

On the easy side: it is a system that makes sense. More important, it makes as much sense on the shop floor as in the executive suites. No longer are you, the boss, in the position of informing employees that now you want them really to think about quality, or that this year you're going to have to cut those budgets, or that reworked costs are spiraling way out of control. No longer do you risk provoking the paralyzing cynicism that greets most directives and initiatives these days. In an open-book company, employees see what's happening and learn how to help move the numbers in the right direction. They also have a reason to care.

To be sure, these three principles are the barest of bones, and I'm sure they provoke as many questions as answers. (You really expect warehouse workers to understand return on assets?) Most of this book is devoted to answering those questions by showing you how open-book management works in the real world. But suspend disbelief for a moment and imagine that you actually could build a company that operated along these lines. As you'll see, this isn't so far-fetched. What you'd have would be an organization that looked, felt, and acted differently from any other company you'd ever seen. Here—in the words of the people who are doing it—are just a few of the things that can happen:

Employees start coming up with productivity-building ideas on their own.

Rick Haarstad, president, Hydraulic Specialty Company (Fridley, Minn.): "We've noticed quite a few improvements! The flow of steel—coming in, getting into racks, and flowing out to work areas in

4

the machine shop—has improved. Our parts room and inventory area have shifted around their shelf space and realigned the aisles to make more room. Our Cedar Rapids branch has put new doors in, to get customers in and out faster.

Our outside sales-and-marketing team and our inside sales group have started to put ventures together to form outside/inside teams for handling their top ten or fifteen accounts. All those improvements have come from the guys making suggestions."

People all over the company begin to watch little costs.

Richard Weiss, president, Mountain Travel Sobek (El Cerrito, Calif.): "Last week someone said, 'Whenever we get a catalog request we send it out first class for $3.00. I think that we should be able to tell from the phone call whether that person needs the catalog in two or three days or whether they can wait a week. Why don't we establish a bulk-mail pool? It would cost $0.77 instead of $3.00. I think 150 is the minimum we'd need to batch, and we probably could get that number in three days. We'd save $2.23 times the number of catalogs—and that would drop right to the bottom line, won't it?'"

Machine operators figure out how to coax ever-greater production from the equipment.

Jim Burrows, production supervisor, gravure pressroom, RR Donnelley & Sons (Northeastern Division, Lancaster, Pa.): "Let's say that the schedule allowed eight hours for makeready on a job. In the past, the press crews felt that as long as they were done in eight hours, they had done a good job. Now they began thinking about ways to do it faster—by bringing out the cylinders ahead of time, for example. People also came to understand the importance of press speed. If they run the press at 25,000 impressions an hour, maybe they can get the job done on schedule. If they figure out how to bump that up to 30,000 impressions an hour, they can cut hours off the job. That creates extra capacity for us, and it allows us to get started on the next job that much sooner."

The numbers move in the right direction.

John DeMaine, president, Carolina Safety Associates (Gastonia, N.C.): "Last year was the first year we really used open-book management, and our profits were up 30 or 40 percent over the year before. It was the most profitable year we've ever had."

Gloria Hale, owner, Hale Glass, Inc. (Anaheim, Calif.): "We have noticed a remarkable, remarkable improvement in our numbers."

William Dee Pickens, founder, Pool Covers Inc. (Richmond, Calif.): "Last year was our highest dollar volume and our highest profit. I attribute most of that growth to open-book management."

People learn to make decisions without involving a manager.
Dan Rothaupt, plant manager, AES Corporation (Uncasville, Conn.): "We have 44 technicians total. They run things. They order parts. Everyone in the plant has the authority to spend the shareholders' money. But they understand the economics of the plant. So when they're making a decision about a broken valve—Should we buy a new one? Should we repair it?—they understand the costs."

Randy Johnson, president, S&R Industries (Baker City, Oreg.): "Our employees get involved in things like our capital expenditure budget for each year, what equipment we need to go out and buy. Some get involved in the estimating and in decision making on matters like insurance policy and profit-sharing policy. A volunteer group of five people runs the suggestion committee. They approve or disapprove the suggestions unless it's a huge dollar item, and they tell me at the end of the month what they did and what price they got. It's one less monkey on my back! That's the whole reason management here is into open-book management: it pushes decisions back down the ladder."

People gain a better understanding of constraints and opportunities.
Chuck Mayhew, president, Foldcraft Company (Kenyon, Minn.): "We know that we can't schedule more than $105,000 worth of product to ship in a given day. If we schedule more than that, we quickly learn what the expediting cost really is—overtime, quality problems, and so on. That affects the books, and people in the organization understand it. They may not like that max number, but they understand it."

Everybody pulls together in a crisis.
Dan Kaplan, cofounder, Anchor Communications (Providence, R.I.): "We came down to the last week of the year and we were off our cash-flow target by $95,000. But all that week people had been putting together ideas to get the money in the door. On the very last day of the year, we collected $105,000. We called up clients,

asking, 'How would you like to prepay your advertising and we'll give you a discount?' And a lot of times the employees were running off to clients to collect checks. I remember when the Federal Express guy came in here with three packages. Well, people ran to greet him—you'd think he was bringing Christmas presents! They tore them open, and there were checks inside. So to me it was a clear example: if you get everyone together on a problem, and you don't hide anything, thirty people can really make it happen!"

This list could go on for a while. Chris LaBarge, president of LaBarge Products Inc. in St. Louis, reports that open-book management forced his company to improve its cost-accounting system because people suddenly realized that it was providing inaccurate information. Bob Taylor, general manager of the heavy-oil business unit of Amoco Canada, in Calgary, Alberta, says that it forced Amoco Canada's managers to understand their business unit's numbers, rather than simply relying on whatever the accounting department came up with. Many other managers related that open-book management took the emotion out of a lot of decisions. "Any time anybody wants to buy something, we break it down: what is it going to cost you each month, and what is it going to make you each month?" explains Lynn Thompson, president of Thompson Pontiac GMC Cadillac, a dealership in Springfield, Missouri. "We use the financial statements to make our decisions, with no personalities involved."

And many, many open-book leaders report that it put the excitement and fun back into business. Carolyn Chandler, owner of a property-management company in San Francisco, is typical. "It used to be that I'd go out, get some new business, then come back and tell the troops, 'We have a fabulous building—200 units.' They'd say, 'Oh, that's nice.' Now I come back and tell them we have a new building and they're clapping and hooting and cheering! Everybody's excited when we get new business."

At any rate, what's important here isn't so much the specifics, it's the common theme. We're all in this together. We can see what's going on, and we have the tools we need to affect what happens. Most important, *whatever benefits the business benefits us all.* That's about as different from what happens in most companies as you can get.

Of course, open-book management isn't any kind of panacea. It doesn't suddenly make everybody in a company get along with everybody else. It can't fix a company that is pursuing the wrong strategy. What it does do is cut down on the gossip, internal politics, mistrust, resentment, and just plain bad management that plague most companies. It reminds people that they're on the same big team, playing the competition, rather than on a little in-house team trying to ace out that other department or put one over on management or cover its rear end in a crisis.

"How do you make a group of several hundred people into one big happy family?" asks Terry Fulwiler, CEO of Wisconsin Label Company in Algoma, Wisconsin. "You have them all have their eye on one common goal, so that everybody's pushing for the same thing, which is to make the company do better."

First Principle: The Transparent Company

Overview: The Importance (and Unimportance) of Numbers

Most businesses are anything but transparent, even in this age of instant communication. They keep a tight lock on critical business information. They expect senior managers to keep strategic plans and financial data to themselves. They tell middle managers only what someone has decided they need to know. And what happens? Employees labor in an informational twilight. They're only dimly aware of how their business unit is doing, whether their department is on budget, when that new product will make it out the door, or how well the latest marketing initiative is paying off. Of course, employees are people, not automatons, and they like to know what's going on. So—like Kremlinologists in the days of the Soviet Union—they pore over snippets of information in hopes of figuring out where the next threats and opportunities lie. Everybody gossips. Everybody spreads rumors. In the absence of real data, the air in a company is filled with speculation and half-truths.

Companies practicing open-book management take the opposite approach. They operate on what might be called the commando-team principle. This is a phrase coined in a completely different context by Tufts University professor Daniel C. Dennett, a philosopher who no doubt will be surprised to find his words borrowed for a business book.* Members of commando teams are told as much as possible about their missions, observes Dennett, so that "the team has a chance of ad-libbing appropriately when unanticipated obstacles arise." Hence the commando-team principle. If

---

Kinds of Minds (New York: Basic Books, 1996) p.131.

you want people to adapt to changing circumstances, make sure they understand the big picture.

Employees of open-book companies are business commandos. They see, and learn to understand, all the relevant data affecting their business unit: financials, key operational numbers, budgets, forecasts, strategic plans, and so forth. Not only does all this knowledge help people adapt to new circumstances quickly, it also helps them understand where they're going, so they can help the company along rather than get in the way.

How do you create a company in which people *can* see and understand what's going on? The next four chapters lay out the fundamentals. First, you figure out—and focus on—the numbers that are critical to *your* business's success (Chapter 3). You prepare financials that people can actually understand and use, week in and week out, on the job (Chapter 4). You develop scoreboards to keep all these numbers out in front of people (Chapter 5), and you give people a chance to learn some business basics, so that they'll have the tools they need to understand the scoreboards (Chapter 6).

First, though, take a moment to consider the importance— and unimportance—of numbers in business.

Business is indisputably a game of numbers. Over the long haul a company's success is measured by its financial performance, period. In the short run, it's measured by numbers that are thought to contribute to that long-run financial performance: sales and earnings growth, share of the market, new products and services introduced, customer satisfaction. Anyone who wants to know how successful a company is, or how successful it's likely to be in the future, looks at the numbers.

Numbers are no less important inside a company. Internal metrics show units shipped, customers served, beds or seats or tables occupied, labor productivity, time required for order entry and delivery. They indicate who's making the budget and who isn't. They show profitability by product line, by location, by division. The numbers alert managers to problems and opportunities. They guide decisions about the allocation of resources.

In short, there is no substitute for *managing by the numbers.* A businessperson who thinks that numbers don't matter is in the wrong line of work. On the other hand, that shopworn phrase conceals two critical issues. It doesn't tell you *which* numbers among the many that a business cranks out each day are the most important. And it doesn't tell you *how* to manage by the numbers. If you're going to pursue open-book management, you need to think about both issues.

Ask an audience of businesspeople which number is ultimately most important to their company, and you're likely to hear "profits" or "the bottom line" from at least half. (Most of the others—particularly if they work for a large company—will say, "making budget.") But a simpleminded focus on profits is just that: simpleminded. Do you mean return on sales? On assets? On equity? Are you looking at profit dollars or profitability? And what about sales growth? Or building shareholder value? If your company is young or fast growing, what about cash flow?

Figuring out the appropriate balance among all these possible objectives is one task facing company owners and senior managers. Figuring out how to reach the objectives is another. If the goal for the moment is boosting return on sales, what variables drive this measure of profitability? How can managers best pursue that objective without making a company vulnerable to a change in the market?

The next chapter, on critical numbers, will return to these questions. They're important to open-book management because when you open the books people need to know which numbers are most important and why.

How you manage by the numbers is equally important. It's easy, for example, to use numbers as a club: just browbeat managers who don't make their objectives. Usually, of course, the club-wielding is subtler. A unit's expenses run high. A plant has a bad month. Suddenly budgets are being cut, investments curtailed, warnings issued. In many, many companies, not making your numbers is still a surefire route to trouble.

When numbers are used as a club, however, one or all of the following happen. The people responsible for the numbers beat up on their subordinates, creating a climate of fear. They focus on the numbers that are being watched and forget all the other numbers that might contribute to business success. Sometimes they fudge the numbers completely; or, like a lot of managers, they just find ways to avoid the scrutiny. A while ago, I was talking with a company VP who was grousing about the folks from corporate headquarters. Before the start of every year, he said, he would negotiate the plant's budget with corporate. As soon as the year began, the accounting department would start issuing its routine forecasts, which, "because everybody wants to be conservative," usually predicted that sales wouldn't be up to budget. At that point, he said, corporate would issue a directive: cut your expenses. No money for training. No money for new investment. "Of course, you can't run a business without doing training and without investing. So then you have to find the money from somewhere else, without corporate knowing."

But numbers don't have to be used as a club. Remember this formula: *people before numbers*. People need to understand why particular numbers are important. People need to be able to take joint responsibility for them. And people need to reap the rewards of making the numbers move in the right direction. You'll note that I have just laid out the principles of open-book management. *Open-book management is a method for managing by the numbers without fear and intimidation.* And a transparent company is one in which numbers are everywhere, and in which people see and use the numbers every day.

The Four Fears

When I talk to people about this principle of building a transparent company, I hear four fears over and over.

Some owners of private companies are, well, aghast. I might as well propose transparent clothing. One actually likened opening his company's books to "dropping your shorts." Another said bluntly that the single toughest thing about open-book management was getting mentally prepared to open the books. People have asked me if they have to show employees their tax returns. They have argued that opening the books compromises their economic privacy.

Alas, there really isn't a good way around this problem. You have to go right through it—or not. If you own your own business and you truly believe that opening your company's books will compromise your privacy, then please do me a favor. Close this book. Give it to a friend. Go back to the old way of running things. Otherwise, get yourself mentally prepared. Hundreds of chief executives have done so; it really won't be as hard as you think. As for that tax return, well, what goes on your tax return is between you, your accountant, and the IRS. Tax-return accounting bears only a faint resemblance to real-world accounting, and not many people run their businesses according to the numbers that appear on their tax returns.

Managers of public companies have a different concern: they fear that they'll get in trouble with the Securities and Exchange Commission by releasing financial information internally. This is an issue that merits scrutiny (and consultation with a lawyer). But many public companies do practice open-book management. Some, such as Physician Sales & Service, a distributor of medical supplies with branches throughout the United States, keep branch-level (or plant-level) books open all the time but release consolidated financials to employees only when they are released to the public. Others, such as AES Corporation, an independent power producer that is traded on the New York Stock Exchange, declare all their employees insiders for stock-trading purposes. AES president Dennis Bakke explains how his company chose this option:

> We faced this question in 1991, when we went public. We asked ourselves: "What's more important to us, sharing information with employees? Or running afoul of securities laws?" Well, we chose to treat our people like real people by sharing all the information. Once you get to that point of view—and it does take time—lawyers and managers and employees have to sit down to figure out how you're going to make it work.
>
> First, you have to tell your lawyer and the Securities and Exchange Commission what you want to do. We talked with our lawyers and said, "This is the way we want to operate our business, by sharing critical information as often as possible. How do we continue to do that and be public?" Some said: "Nah, that's impossible." But we considered the options and guidelines and concluded that we could do it if everybody were treated as an insider. I thought it was a nifty idea and a workable solution. Back then, we had only about 450 employees. Today we're well over 5,000.
>
> Anyway, once we had our options, we went around to our people and said, "Hey, we have this choice: if everybody's an insider, we can buy and sell shares of AES only during open periods, not during closed periods." Although many employees liked to trade their shares freely, they decided they'd rather be insiders. And we've had no trouble since. We have all kinds of fancy communications that go out when the trading window closes. In the home office, we have a universal "no stock" symbol—the word *stock* with a circle and a line through it. There are some regular times we close the window, and people have become accustomed to when those times are. We'll also close it when some significant company event may be happening. For example, when we won this big deal in Brazil.

Since 100 percent of our people own AES shares, it concerns everyone. But everybody wants the information. They want to be insiders. You just have to trust that everybody will follow the rules. Maybe you have to deal with an exception when something happens, but we haven't encountered that yet. And it's been five years.

Companies shouldn't be afraid of this. It's no big deal. And I think it's a great motivator for people. They know they're important. Important people are insiders.

The third fear in this open-book list of terrors has to do with the competition: management believes that if employees know the numbers, surely the competition will find out.

I think this fear is overblown. Open-book companies trust their employees with information that may be sensitive. Most people respond responsibly to that kind of trust, particularly if they understand the reasons for it. But even if one disgruntled employee spills the beans, so what? Chances are your competitors know most of your numbers anyway. And chances are you'd be better off focusing on your customers than on your competitors.

Besides, employees are trusted with sensitive information every day. They work with proprietary equipment and software. They work on confidential projects. Business law provides a variety of protections—noncompete and nondisclosure agreements, for instance—against leaking trade secrets and spilling company-specific information. These protections don't always work, granted. On the other hand, you can't ask people to work with a blindfold on.

The last fear touches so sensitive a nerve that it comes up in nearly every preliminary conversation about what open-book management involves: Does opening the books mean that everybody knows everybody else's salary?

I know some open-book practitioners who absolutely insist that, yup, it means just that, and if you're not ready for it, buster, you're not ready for open-book management. I'm sympathetic to that stance; everybody gossips about everybody else's salary anyway, so there's something to be said for getting the information out on the table. Also, getting it out there forces the issue of fairness, which is what lies behind most of the gossip. In an ideal world, we'd all know how much each other was paid and wouldn't really care, because it would all seem fair and equitable.

Ultimately, though, I don't agree that open-book management has to involve public disclosure of what everybody makes. This isn't an ideal world. Most companies' pay scales are a jumble of seniority, skills, special deals, historical accidents, favoritism, and bureaucratic rules. They aren't fair by anyone's definition. Publicizing everyone's wage or salary is a recipe for trouble. Besides, it just isn't essential for everybody to know everybody else's pay. The important thing in open-book management is the company's numbers, not individuals' compensation. Salaries or wage costs can be lumped together so that no one need know exactly what the project engineers or the customer-service reps or the machinists make. And this is how most companies practice open-book management.

So let's assume you're persuaded and you want to create a transparent company. The next chapters show you how.

Critical Numbers

The first step in building a transparent company is to figure out your business's critical numbers. Critical numbers are the numbers that determine a company's success.

Note that I said the numbers that *determine* success, not the numbers that *measure* success. Conventional indicators, such as net profit or return on assets, may or may not be critical numbers. And anyway, your critical numbers are likely to change over time.

I'd better explain.

For starters, I have to say that I didn't think up the idea of critical numbers. It comes from Jack Stack, CEO of Springfield ReManufacturing Corporation, author (with Bo Burlingham) of *The Great Game of Business* (which you should also read if you haven't already), and a person who has probably done more than any other individual on the planet to develop and popularize the ideas of open-book management. Springfield ReManufacturing Corporation, known as SRC, got its start in 1983, when Stack and a dozen colleagues bought out what was then a troubled engine-remanufacturing facility owned by International Harvester (now Navistar). This was the mother of all leveraged buyouts, at least if your emphasis is on the word *leveraged*. Stack and his associates came up with about $100,000 in equity. They borrowed $8.9 million of the $9 million purchase price, at rates that these days would be considered usury. Their debt-to-equity ratio was 89 to 1.

And what was SRC's critical number in those early years? Simple: it was that debt-to-equity ratio. If SRC didn't generate enough cash to pay off its bank debt, it was out of business. Sales growth, productivity, profitability, quality—all those numbers meant nothing except insofar as they contributed to the company's ability to reduce its debt and build its equity.

So this is the first way of looking at critical numbers. It's an approach that Stack uses frequently when he's explaining the concept.

A critical number is a number that, if it moves in the wrong direction, means a company's very survival is in jeopardy.

For a lot of young businesses, cash is a critical number in this sense. You can run a company without profits for a while, but you can't run it for more than a *very* short time without cash. Turnarounds, start-ups, fast-growing companies, many tiny family-owned businesses—none can take for granted an adequate supply of cash, so they have to watch it like a hawk. No cash, no business.

But there are plenty of numbers other than cash-flow figures that can indicate potentially life-threatening situations for a company. For retailers, sales per square foot and inventory turns are likely to be handy indicators of potential trouble. For restaurants, movie theaters, hotels, hospitals, cruise operators, and airlines, the critical number for survival is percentage of seats (or beds) filled. If you're consistently below your break-even occupancy rate, you know you have to do something fast. For service businesses, the make-or-break critical number is often billable hours, or the ratio of billable hours to total hours. For newspapers and magazines, it's advertising revenues.

Manufacturing companies typically have to watch several numbers at once. Even so, every manufacturer knows the importance to survival of one basic number, namely, a plant's break-even level of operation. Stack tells of a friend who owned a gear-manufacturing company and every morning wanted to know the weight of the gears that had been shipped the previous day. That number was a rough-and-ready measure of the plant's throughput. If it "unexpectedly fell below a certain level, he could quickly zero in on the problem and make sure it got fixed."*

A company's critical number in this sense is a kind of gate; you have to reach, and stay at, a certain level, or you don't get to stay in business. "The critical number is the number that can take out an organization" if it moves in the wrong way, says Stack.

---

*"The Logic of Profit," *Inc.*, March 1996, p. 17.

But most established businesses aren't in danger of going broke. They're already beyond that gate. And for them, the concept of critical numbers has another kind of meaning.

> Critical numbers are the numbers that drive a business's key objectives. They're the numbers that must move in the right direction if the business is to succeed in what it is trying to do *right now.*

This is why a company's critical numbers can change from time to time. During start-up—or during a turnaround like SRC's—a business's key objective may be simply to generate enough cash to stay alive. At other times a key objective may be to lower costs, or expand market share, or boost customer satisfaction. A company that needs process reengineering may decide that this year a key objective is to reduce throughput time or to increase labor productivity. A company too dependent on a single customer may decide that diversification is a key objective over the next two years. In some periods of their lives companies focus more on eliminating weaknesses. In other periods they focus more on pursuing opportunities. Critical numbers can flow from both kinds of objectives.

Determining Your Critical Numbers
Step One: Strategic planning

There's a moral lurking here, which is that you can't figure out your critical numbers if you don't know your objectives. Critical numbers tell you if you're getting where you want to go—but first you have to know where you're going. So the first step in mapping out your critical numbers is to determine your company's goals.

Most businesses refer to this process as strategic planning. Large organizations have whole departments devoted to it; they produce multiyear, multivolume plans, which, as often as not, wind up gathering dust on executives' shelves. In small companies the strategic plan, insofar as there is one, often resides in the owner's head. This isn't a book on strategic planning, so I'm not going to devote a lot of space to the topic. But open-book management depends on a clear plan, so it can't be avoided either. Here are the basics.

Strategic planning has to be an active, explicit process. If the plan sits on the shelf, or if it sits unexamined (and unexpressed) in the owner's head, it's worthless. A strategic plan has value only if it serves as a guide to action—only, in other words, if people in a company *know* what the objectives are.

It also has to be a dynamic process. The market no longer holds still for a five-year—or, in some industries, even a three-year—strategic plan. Typically, companies do a rolling three-year plan, revisiting it every year. They also make a point of examining the plan every quarter to see if its parameters and objectives still make sense.

The three key inputs to a strategic plan are (1) an understanding of the company's mission and competencies; (2) market intelligence; and (3) an understanding of the plan's financial dimension. You can't build an effective plan unless you know what your company is *about*—what its mission in the marketplace is and what it can and cannot do well. Nor can you build an effective plan unless you understand what's happening in your industry, including the strengths and weaknesses of your competitors, how customers' tastes or preferences may be changing, what technological innovations may lie on the horizon, and so on.

Finally, you must understand the plan's financial ramifications. You can't plan for breakneck sales growth, for instance, without also planning to ensure a sufficient supply of cash. You probably don't want to plan for record-breaking profits if that means giving short shrift to product development. My friend Bill Fotsch, a consultant who works with Jack Stack and SRC, points out that good strategic planning is holistic: it sets out objectives for a year or two years or five years, but it puts these objectives in a framework, rather than focusing on one or two goals without taking into account their impact on other aspects of a company's operation.

The objectives set by a strategic plan have to be tailored to an appropriate time frame. You can reengineer a business process, and thereby boost labor productivity, in six months. You may need several years to attain a goal of, say, 50 percent of total revenue from new products or services. A good strategic plan includes both long-term and short-term goals. But whatever the overall time frame, *this year's* strategic plan should include measurable objectives, or steps toward a later objective, that can be attained in a year.

Good strategic planning is an iterative process that involves building consensus. Smart companies involve as many people as possible in planning—not just the management team, but employees at all levels of the organization. (This is a theme we'll come back to later.) They set up procedures to gather information and opinions from frontline employees and supervisors. What do you think? What are you hearing about the marketplace? Where are the weaknesses in your area? Ultimately, senior management has to set a company's direction. But top managers' decisions are likely to be better if they've gotten input from a lot of other people. And a company's employees are more likely to buy into, and support, objectives that they have had a hand in setting.

Step Two: Focusing on performance drivers

Once the objectives for the next time period are in place, the task is to figure out and home in on the operational and financial variables—*performance drivers*—that show whether you're on the right track.

Sometimes this process is pretty simple. Let's say you own your own restaurant. You're not really worried about long-term diversification or product development; your goal is simply to maximize pretax profit over the course of a year. To maximize profits you need to bring in a lot of customers, charge them enough to permit healthy margins, and watch your costs so that those margins don't somehow evaporate. Along the way you'll have to make decisions about what to serve, what to charge, how many people to hire, where to buy your food, and so on.

You can capture the impact of these decisions in a few key ratios—so the ratios, in effect, *drive* your business along the road toward its objectives. One such ratio is percentage of tables filled. Two more are food costs and labor costs as a percentage of sales. Veteran restaurant owners may hardly have to consult the actual figures, because they have an intuitive grasp of the reality that is expressed in the ratios. But if you're looking for numbers to watch, ratios such as these will ultimately determine your profitability.

Often a given objective may have multiple or even contradictory drivers; then managers have to figure out which drivers warrant the company's focus. Return on sales, for example, can be increased by boosting average gross margin or decreasing overhead expenses relative to sales volume. Company A may decide to boost average gross margin by cutting its sales volume (or slowing the pace of growth), so as to focus on the most profitable customers. Company B—with the same overall objective—may focus on increasing sales so as to reduce overhead.

Step Three: Identifying *this year's* opportunities or weaknesses

In the long term, any number of variables may be important to a business's success. That restaurant, for instance, needs a good location; if it's a high-class place, it will need a great chef. In the short term, though—meaning over the 12 months that are covered in the typical strategic plan—many of the variables that determine success won't change. Some, such as lease payments, may not even be controllable. So your critical numbers will be the ones that you can affect—the ones that you can move in the right direction *this year*.

How to find them? One method is to identify your company's key weaknesses. Gather up data on your competitors and on your industry in general. Talk to lenders, investors, customers. Maybe your production costs are higher than they should be, or your sales per square foot lower. Maybe your inventory accuracy is poor, or inventory turns low. Maybe your projects are consistently coming in over budget. Any of these metrics can be critical numbers if they represent problems that you want (or need) to address this year.

A second method is to focus on key opportunities. Where are the avenues for growth? If you want to expand into a new market, a critical number might be percentage of revenues derived from that market. If you think you can prosper just by doing more of what you're doing, good old-fashioned sales growth can be a critical number. The point is to agree on a measurable goal or goals. If the goal can't be expressed in numbers, you'll have no way of knowing how you're progressing toward it.

Step Four: A *cascade* of critical numbers

The larger the organization, the more critical numbers you need, if only because a larger number of people and departments affect the company's overall performance. But these numbers should cascade from the company's (or business unit's) overall critical numbers. They should bear an understandable relationship to the organization's goals, and they should be measurable in financial terms.

Suppose, for example, that one of the goals people in your company agree on is 10 percent sales growth with steady return on sales (RoS). That would increase profit dollars and (presumably) contribute to an increase in share value. That goal alone can spawn critical numbers for nearly everyone:

- Sales and marketing people have to bring in the extra 10 percent. They'll need to figure out where it's going to come from (which products, which customers), when and how they can bring it in, and whether they'll need additional resources to realize the goal. They won't be able to sacrifice much in the way of margin, unless other departments can provide equivalent savings. *Critical numbers: sales volume, gross margin.*

- In a manufacturing operation, purchasing and production people have to determine how to generate the additional output. Will there be bottlenecks or cost pressures in parts and materials? Is there a need for additional equipment? How much more labor will be required and where will it come from? *Critical numbers: cost of goods sold (COGS) as a percentage of sales,* along with whatever numbers are most important in determining that ratio (e.g., labor productivity).

- Customer-service and other staff departments will need to support the additional 10 percent in sales, including support for whatever additional personnel may be required. Can they hold general and administrative (G&A) costs steady, thus giving salespeople some leeway on margin, or at least increase them less than 10 percent? Can cash be utilized more efficiently than in the past? *Critical numbers: G&A as a percentage of sales* (and the budget line items that make up G&A); *key accounting ratios* (such as receivable days).

What's important here isn't so much the specifics, which vary widely from company to company, it's the idea that *everybody's* critical numbers contribute to the same set of objectives. Incidentally, this is really the only way of putting some teeth in that perennial managerial refrain, We've got to control our costs. When people see where the costs show up and how they affect a company's financial performance, the logic of cost control becomes that much more powerful.

How to Screw Up

Critical numbers aren't magic; they can lead a company astray as well as give it a boost. Some common errors:

1. **Poor strategic planning.** A company sets out to increase gross margins. Marketers and salespeople dutifully concentrate on

old, high-margin products and neglect newer but lower-margin products. Result: the company grows increasingly dependent on yesterday's wares.

2. **Identifying the wrong drivers.** Jack Stack tells the story of the hotel manager who wanted to increase profits by controlling expenses. Trouble was, he wasn't filling enough rooms to make money no matter how low his operating costs. "His real critical number was his occupancy rate."

3. **Relying on bad information.** A large service company wants to reduce the unit cost of delivering its service, so it shuts down small, apparently inefficient, regional offices and transfers their functions to bigger cities. Only later does it discover the smaller offices were actually the low-cost deliverers. (This really happened.)

4. **The number nobody understands.** "One company decided its critical number was economic value added (EVA)," reports Bill Fotsch. "They weren't wrong—that measure reflected a lot of what they needed to do. But no one got it! They went a year and nothing happened."

5. **Forgetting business objectives.** On-time delivery is a great metric—until it pushes costs so far up that you're no longer competitive. Critical numbers make sense when they support business objectives, not when they undermine them.

6. **Premature self-congratulations.** You do industry comparisons and find that your return on sales is high, so you think there's no need for critical-number analysis? Look again. Maybe competitors are spending twice as much on R&D as you are. You have to identify weaknesses, not just strengths.

Using Your Critical Numbers

Using numbers in running a business is a fundamental theme of open-book management. We'll be returning to it throughout this book, notably in the sections on accountability and games. For the moment, though, just think about the possibilities inherent in identifying a few critical numbers that are directly related to a company's goals.

- You could begin talking to employees about those numbers, explaining why they're important and how people throughout the company can have an impact on them. Suddenly people can begin to see how *they* make a difference to the company's success.

- You could track the numbers regularly and publicly (see Chapter 5 on scoreboards). Suddenly the company's performance becomes a kind of game. How did we do last month? How are we doing this month?

- You could ask employees to help set a goal for the critical numbers over the course of the next month, quarter, or year, with a bonus or some other kind of reward if they make the goal. Suddenly people have set themselves a challenge—and nobody likes to fail in a challenge, especially one a person's established for himself or herself. Next step: brainstorming about *how* to move the numbers.

- You could ask people to forecast their numbers; to predict where they will be at the end of each week or month as they move toward the goal. When people have to forecast, two things happen, both good. First, they have to be sure they understand what makes the number move. Otherwise they'll have no basis on which to forecast. Second, they learn how to manage the number over time. That feedback loop—predict, watch what happens, predict again, experiment, see what happens again—is one of the most powerful teaching experiences there is.

What you would be doing with all these steps is beginning to change the way people think about business and about their jobs.

A company, after all, is an organization with a purpose. It provides goods or services that people want. It generates wealth for its owners and employees. The company's critical numbers show how it is doing. As Jack Stack would put it, they show whether the company is winning The Great Game of Business.

The sad thing about most jobs is that the connection between people's work and that overall purpose is so remote. There's no understanding of the game, let alone of how to keep score. How many times have you pulled into a gas station or walked into a store, only to be served by a bored or sullen employee who (you can tell) would just as soon you had entered somebody else's establishment? Yet here you are—a customer! With money to spend! When your money goes into the register, it affects the business's financial performance. Sales go up. Inventory is consumed. It becomes a little easier for the company to make a profit this month. Suppose employees could understand and track all that? Suppose they knew that if they hit a certain goal, there would be something in it for them? A company needs employees who feel as enthusiastic and excited about serving a customer as a fledgling shopkeeper on the very first day the shop is open for business. It needs employees who worry as much about a business's weaknesses—a cash-flow crunch, say—as does the man or woman whose name is on the bank loan.

When you identify and communicate critical numbers, this actually begins to happen.

At a small retailing chain in California the goal one year was to achieve a 15 percent increase in every store's sales. If the company achieved this objective, everybody would get a bonus. How to boost sales? Well, two of the numbers that needed to move in the right direction were (1) daily customer count and (2) average sale per customer. These were numbers that nearly every salesclerk could affect. Salesclerks could encourage friends and relatives to shop at the store. They could help make customers aware of sales and other special deals. Above all, they could make sure that every customer who came in the door went away satisfied. To help keep employees focused on those numbers, the human resources manager posted big charts and organized monthly contests with small prizes. (Employees of a store that beat its average-sale-per-customer goal for the month might win a lottery ticket or a silver dollar.) Pretty soon, people were taking register readings a couple of times a day to see how they were doing. Working the floor was no longer just a chore; it had a purpose.

At Anchor Communications, publisher of the magazine *Rhode Island Monthly*, the goal one year was to resolve a cash-flow problem. "At the time," explains cofounder Dan Kaplan, "we had a $200,000 line of credit—and our CFO was projecting a year-end negative cash balance of $350,000." Suddenly Anchor's goal was solvency, and its critical number was the balance in the company's checking account. Kaplan reports what happened next:

> First we introduced the staff, in a group meeting, to what cash flow is all about. We showed them all of the numbers. And we said we need to develop a plan. We'll need everybody's

ideas on how we can not only not arrive at –$350,000 but also try to get up the line of credit to zero by year's end.

We had a lot of fun! People participated. One of the things we did was to set up a little game. We asked them to guess the bank balance as of December 29—the last day of the year. And if we were in positive territory, everybody would get a $50 restaurant gift certificate. The person who came closest to guessing the bank balance would get a $1,500 travel gift certificate. So everybody really got on board. We updated everybody along the way. We had charts all around. It was all very striking.

Well, we came down to the last week of the year, and my thought was, "This was really dumb." We were off our target by $95,000. But all that week, people put together those ideas about how to get money in the door. On the very last day of the year, we collected $105,000.

Anchor wound up the year cash positive.

Real-World Critical Numbers

To help you think about your own company's critical numbers, here's how a few companies analyze and use critical numbers.

A craft production shop.
Bill Palmer, president, Commercial Casework Inc. (Fremont, Calif.): "We manufacture and install architectural cabinetry. We're in a labor-intensive, tight-margin industry, so gross margin is the name of the game for us. A little improvement in gross margin—which we can get by completing our jobs on or under budget—makes an enormous difference. On the other hand, you can have the best margin in the world, but if you don't have the sales volume, it doesn't do you any good. And if you end the year with a great sales volume and great margin but no backlog, that doesn't do you any good either.

"So those are our three critical numbers: gross margin, sales volume, and backlog. Everybody can affect those numbers, so we make sure everybody sees them. And we pay our bonus based on targets for those numbers."

An oil-and-gas exploration company.
Fred Plummer, progress coordinator, Amoco Canada (Calgary, Alberta): "For us, operating expense is one critical number, because it directly impacts the bottom line. But in large companies, expenses

tend to get lumped together where nobody can see them. We've been relentless on cost control for years—you have to be in this industry—but sometimes people have been focusing on small costs while ignoring big ones.

"Now we're beginning to show people exactly where each cost shows up on the income statement, and how much it is. Then they can take responsibility for the numbers that they control. Let's say we want to reduce the cost of vehicles driven by plant service technicians. The technicians would brainstorm ways to reduce those costs, and come up with a performance improvement plan. Then they'd chart their progress, and they could see whether the savings were actually showing up on the operating expenses line of their unit's income statement. If it made a difference, they'd know they were helping the business make money. If it didn't, they'd know that they needed to come up with a new approach."

An inbound-call customer-service center.

Edie Heilman, president, Share Commercial Services Inc. (San Francisco): "We have four key drivers of our financial success. One is abandonment rate. We are paid by the number of calls we handle, at least that's the lion's share of the revenue we bring in, so when we abandon calls we automatically lose revenue. Right now we're targeting a 5 percent rate, but eventually we need to get much lower. A second driver is our sales conversion rate. For a sales call we're not paid for just answering the call, we're only paid for turning it into a sale. Our goal is a 40 percent conversion rate, which is a stretch.

"The third driver is win-backs—getting former customers back. We have a goal for that, too. And the last one is calls per paid hour. Paid hours are literally all the hours we pay for, on the phone and off the phone, here and on vacation. So this makes us manage our people better. What we need to do is fit the hours that people work best with the call volumes. This is tricky. In an inbound call center, you never know when that call volume is going to surge. But it's a measure that all the customer-service reps can understand: if I worked eight hours today and took 60 calls, how many calls am I taking for every hour I'm paid?"

A manufacturing facility.

Jim Siegel, plant manager, Hexacomb Corporation (Trenton, Ill., facility): "For us, the critical number is the ratio of shipments to budgeted sales. We post the numbers on the board every day—

what orders we're getting in, what we have shipped to date, what we're budgeted for. People know that once we hit 100 percent of budget, the bottom line is going to swell. At 110 percent it's going to be a big, fat month. In this business, output is really up to the operators. How fast they run depends on how quickly they can change over from one job to another, how fast they can get the machines up to maximum speed, where they deploy people, and so forth. It's a matter of minutes here, minutes there. They watch the number and know what they have to do."

An auto dealership.

Dale Critz Jr., vice president and general manager, Critz Inc. (Savannah, Ga.): "Our objective is to boost return on assets. That means increasing net profits and managing our assets better. Everyone in the dealership can contribute to these numbers somehow. Salespeople can sell more cars and get the inventories turned faster. Service technicians can be sure they're billing for as many hours as possible. The nice thing is that people see how everything is interconnected. When we sell a car, for example, we'll often arrange financing for a customer as an agent of a bank or a finance company. The faster we get that contract to them, the faster we get our money. But if the salesperson hasn't collected all the information we need at the time we deliver the car, the contract gets held up. This shows up in our financials as a special receivable called 'contracts in transit.' If we can lower that number, it means we're getting our cash faster, which lets us pay down our line of credit on our inventory. Our expenses are lower, so return on assets goes up."

Financials You Can
Actually Use

Critical numbers provide a kind of handy, heads-up display of a company's health. They allow managers and employees to see at a glance how they're doing, whether they're on track toward their goals, or whether they're running into trouble. Over the long run, though, a business's health and success are measured not by just a few critical numbers but by the complete financials: the income statement, the balance sheet, the cash-flow statement, plus all the individual metrics and ratios contained in these documents. If you can read them, the financials provide a comprehensive CAT scan of a company. They reveal internal strengths and weaknesses. They show how a company's performance stacks up against others. They tell people whether a company is worth investing in or lending money to and how secure its jobs are. The financials are the only set of measurements that can not only capture the big picture but render it transparent. In principle, they tell managers (and employees) whether the moves they're making are working or whether they need to try something else.

I say "in principle" because not many people in the average company really do use the financials as a guide to figuring out what to do.

How could they? Typically, only a few senior managers—in some small companies, only the owner—have regular access to financial reports. Outside the accounting department, they're the only individuals likely to have the training and experience necessary to know what all the numbers mean.

But even the folks running an organization may not use the financials much. The documents are complex. The numbers reflect accounting conventions, not necessarily the reality of what goes on inside an organization. How many managers keep handwritten cheat-sheet data in a desk drawer because they don't believe the numbers that issue from accounting? "When I was at GE and going from operation to operation trying to figure out how to improve performance," writes Jerry McAdams in *The Reward Plan Advantage*, "I discovered the 'center drawer' rule of success. I would walk into a manager's office that was piled high with green and white computer paper in fat blue binders and say, 'How's it going?' Instead of going to those mounds of data for an answer, the manager would inevitably go to the center desk drawer. He would then pull out an envelope or scrap of paper with four or five numbers scribbled on it and say, 'Pretty good.'"*

Then, too, a company's financials by definition tell what happened last month, last quarter, last year. Managers are usually too concerned with what's happening right now—and what's likely to happen tomorrow—to give them more than a cursory glance.

So step two in the process of building a transparent company is to create financial reports that do what financials are supposed to do: reveal the information that managers and employees need in order to know how they're doing.

One dimension of this task is well beyond the scope of this book (not to mention the scope of my expertise) and applies to every company, not just to those practicing open-book management. Your financials have to be *good*. They have to reflect what's really going on, so that those cheat sheets become unnecessary. Costs have to be determined accurately, and overhead allocated in a way that makes sense. The numbers can't be compromised by real-world screwups, such as lousy inventory accuracy. Your financials also have to be *complete*. Some companies manage by the income statement and forget that a P&L alone can't tell them how well they're managing their cash or how efficiently they're using their assets. Others live and die by cash flow and never pause to consider the relative profitability of their products and services. A business always needs to be evaluated along three financial dimensions: profitability, cash flow, and return on assets (or some other balance-sheet measure). If you aren't using all three metrics—or if you don't understand

---

* *The Reward Plan Advantage* (San Francisco: Jossey-Bass Publishers, 1996), pp. 41–42.

the connections among them—you're not utilizing financial reports to their fullest advantage.*

The other dimensions of the task, however, are directly relevant to open-book companies. The difference between those companies and everybody else, after all, is that they propose to have everyone, not just those at the top, see the financials and use them in doing their jobs. So the financial reports have to be

- *understandable*, and not only to people with training in accounting and finance;

- *timely*, meaning that people get them a whole lot sooner than 30 days after the close of a quarter;

- *unbundled*, providing information not just about a whole company or business unit but about individual departments and processes; and

- *forward looking,* not merely historical, so people can base their actions on what's likely to happen as well as what has already happened.

Wouldn't it be nice to have a set of financials that met these criteria? Open-book companies have gone a long way toward developing exactly that.

Understandable Financials: Simplify!

If people in a company are going to understand its financials, they'll need instruction in the basics—and in the language—of business. (We'll return to this topic in Chapter 6.) But they'll also need reports that focus on the important items without too much extraneous detail. The financial dimension of a business is ultimately a matter of a very simple formula, that is, revenues minus costs equals profit. Accountants necessarily clutter up this simple formula with such items as inventory adjustments and depreciation. But when you're

---

* A device known as the Mobley Matrix shows the precise relationship among all three statements. If you get a chance to take a seminar called "The Financial Game for Decision Making," take it. It explains the Matrix in words even those of us with zero background in accounting can understand. See also *Beyond IBM: Leadership, Marketing, and Finance for the 1990s*, by Lou Mobley and Kate McKeown (Enter Publishing, 1989), especially Chapter 10.

trying to make the operation of a business transparent, you want to keep the clutter to a minimum.

How to do it? Simple. Save the complete financials for your banker and CFO. Prepare a simplified version for distribution. If it's on one page, so much the better.

Foldcraft Company, which makes restaurant and institutional seating in tiny Kenyon, Minnesota, mounted a reengineering effort a couple of years ago. The company redesigned processes such as order entry. It restructured its manufacturing lines, using a principle known as synchronous manufacturing. Foldcraft is a company you'll hear of a lot in this book, because it's been so successful and has such a well-developed open-book system. Thanks to the reengineering, revenue per employee rose 20 percent in one year, cash flow improved fivefold, and inventory turns nearly doubled.

Anyway, as Foldcraft reengineered its processes, it also created a new income statement so that people could understand it more easily. The statement—dubbed the "sync," for synchronous, statement—has only a few lines. "Sales" is whatever is shipped out during a week. "Materials cost" is deducted from sales to give "throughput." Everything else is treated as an expense, with each line item broken down by department. "It really enables the whole organization to understand what's happening," says CFO Doug Westra.

Joe Clark, owner of the Chick-fil-A store at Crossroads Mall in Mount Hope, West Virginia, is another simplifier. Clark and his friend Jim Brown, another Chick-fil-A operator, badly wanted to launch open-book management with their employees, most of whom aren't old enough to vote. Starting out, they gave everybody a detailed, four-page income statement. (Clark winces at the memory: "It was too much!") Today Clark's and Brown's employees get a simplified weekly P&L that shows sales along with ten line items ("food, paper, labor, repairs, cleaning supplies, and so forth"). That basic business equation shows up in a form that even high-school kids can understand.

Of course, you can tailor the financials to your own business. Dale Critz Jr., vice president and general manager of Critz Inc., the auto dealer, reports that his company designed its own income statement: "We have taken three pages of financials and put them on one page. In our business, the four major expense groups are variable expense, which is sales commissions on the cars we sell; personnel expense, including salaries and benefits; semifixed expense, which is items such as advertising, floor-plan interest, data-processing expense, and outside services; and fixed expense, such as rent and utilities. Going across the page, you've got it broken down by department—new cars, used cars, service, parts, and corporate. Everybody can see exactly how their department did." Critz's one-page sheet also includes some balance-sheet elements: inventories, receivables, and contracts-in-transit.

Timely Financials: Weeklies, Dailies, Fast Closes

How long does *your* accounting department take to produce a monthly or quarterly financial report? Most smaller companies still take about two weeks, while larger ones take most of a month. Some of that delay is inevitable, particularly in big companies. But some of it is a relic of old, cumbersome systems and procedures, not to mention outdated expectations about how long an accounting department *should* take to produce reports.

These days, companies with good information systems can close the books weekly. They can produce useful flash reports every day. They can get key monthly performance data into managers' and employees' hands quickly, even if they haven't gone through the full procedure of closing the books (accountants call this a *soft close*). Benchmark your company's performance against these open-book companies:

- Foldcraft Company does a full close every week. "This is a real close," says president Chuck Mayhew. "We actually publish a month-to-date income statement every week. The accounting folks can now close the books in a day and a half. We have 5 accounting people, and 250 employees, and we do that 52 times a year." Foldcraft also prints a report every morning showing "how many orders were placed the day before, the dollar value of those orders, what was shipped the day before, what the margins were on what was shipped, and how many orders that should have gone out but didn't. It's all broken out by market and territory." Managers get the reports first, then the company posts them on bulletin boards. "Everybody in the organization can see exactly where we stand every day."

- Electronic Controls Company, in Boise, Idaho, prepares a simplified income statement every week. This one, according to president Ed Zimmer, isn't a detailed line-item statement; it's more of an overview. "On the normal monthly statement, for example, labor and materials are allocated to product lines, so that people can analyze the performance of their groups. On the weekly statement those numbers are just summarized." ECCO, as the company is known, dubs its weekly statements *flash reports*. "All the managers review them at weekly meetings, and any exceptions—numbers that are over or under plan—have to be explained by the responsible person. We also post it in the factory, so that everybody knows how we're doing every week."

- Mid-States Technical Staffing Services, in Davenport, Iowa, prepares what founder Steve Wilson calls *weekly minifinancials*. "We know the previous week's billings by Monday afternoon. By Tuesday, we'll have a pretty good estimate of last week's direct costs. Then we put in one-quarter of the month's budgeted SG&A, do the arithmetic, and we have a good operational estimate of weekly pretax income. By Wednesday, everyone here knows whether they're on track for the month's profit targets."

- Colonial Mills, in Pawtucket, Rhode Island, has an electronic daily report. "This is a flash report that goes out over E-mail," says company president Don Scarlata. "It has all of the key statistics that we need: incoming orders, shipments, production numbers, our receivables, payables, cash balances, et cetera. We drive off of that. It isn't an accountant's report, but it's live information. The key here is not to wait until two weeks after you close the month to get the financial statements and go, 'Oh, shoot, we should have done *this* in week two,' and now it's six weeks later. What we need to do is get everybody to focus on where are we now and what can we do about it tomorrow!"

Unbundled Financials: By Department, Shift, Machine

Financial reports traditionally apply to whole companies or business units. Staff departments get budgets, production departments get production goals, and no one ever sees how those budgets or goals fit into the organization's overall financial performance. This is another practice that open-book companies, with the help of modern information technology, are throwing out the window. Result:

a lot of minibusinesses inside the organization, each with its own set of financials. The Framingham, Massachusetts, plant of Web Industries provides machine crews with their own monthly P&Ls. Woodpro Cabinetry, in Cabool, Missouri, prepares financial statements for each of its self-governing work teams. Joe Clark, the Chick-fil-A operator, does income statements for each shift.

People in staff and service departments of open-book companies can't get P&Ls in this sense. But they can and do see their budget, track their performance to budget, and learn where the budget fits into the income statement. That alone can create the sense of being "in business." Example? Mid-States Technical Staffing Services allocates a certain amount—determined by the company's overall sales plan—to the corporate staff at the start of the year. "If the corporate staff overspends, they still only get that same allocation," explains Steve Wilson. "So corporate can show a 'loss.' And if they don't spend as much as planned, they generate a 'profit.' This year, my corporate staff is about a $59,000 profit center. Every month they get to pat themselves on the back for that. And that $59,000 goes right to the bottom line."

Forward-Looking Financials: Managing the Future

Every company gets monthly and quarterly financials. Most companies prepare periodic forecasts of the coming quarter or year. And what's the connection between the two? Usually, not much. Forecasting and reviewing the financials are generally undertaken separately. The impact of the forecast on all the numbers that make up the financials is rarely spelled out. In larger companies, forecasts often issue from the accounting department and are ignored by everybody else. In smaller ones, the owner scribbles his or her forecasts on a sheet of paper and sticks it in a desk drawer.

In open-book companies, forecasting is *systematic*. It's done every week or every month, in public, as part of the company's regular review of its financial performance. In the most common model, patterned after the practices developed by Jack Stack at Springfield ReManufacturing Corporation, the company prepares an annual plan, and regular financial-review meetings assess its performance relative to the plan. But managers at those meetings also offer opinions as to how the numbers for which they are responsible may vary during the next month or quarter.

In effect, the company's financial statements look forward as well as backward. Past months show plan and performance. Coming months show plan and opinion. The purpose is to allow managers to address changes and trouble spots as they are happening—and to know what's likely to happen before it actually happens. "If you can forecast your business," says Stack, "you can manage it." At the same time, the public nature of these ever-changing forecasts means that everyone in the company is working from the same information. It's one more step in creating a truly transparent organization.

Here's how it works in other companies:

- At Vectra, a printing and marketing-services company in Columbus, Ohio, the model is very much like SRC's. "We compare plan to actual," says co-owner Mimi Taylor. "We talk about our performance, our operating-income goal, where we are relative to our operating-income goal, where we are to budget. We also have an 'opinion' line, like SRC. Opinion is four weeks out: 'This is what our budget says we're going to do, but here's what the short term looks like.' That way, we can make adjustments if that four weeks doesn't look as good as the budget. And if it looks better, what do we need to do to get ready for that?"

- Foldcraft forecasts the current month at the weekly managers meeting. Chuck Mayhew: "The first week, they're only one week intelligent. By the fourth week they're four weeks intelligent. The reason we do this is not just to be able to say, 'Looks like we're going to make some money this month.' It's to get people thinking about how to control the numbers they're responsible for." Mayhew sounds like Stack in the value he places on forecasting. "I believe if you can predict your numbers correctly, you have a firm understanding of where they're coming from. You know the cause and effect. And once you know cause and effect, you can control it. We want people to think, 'I'm in control. I *know* what I need to do to make that number different.'"

Forecasting isn't just a job for meetings.

- At Web Industries' plant in Framingham, Massachusetts, work teams get so-called road maps at the start of every month. "A road map is essentially projections," explains team leader Rob Zicaro. "It projects sales for the team for the month, with the largest customers listed. As the month progresses, each team member does production reports, and each production report measures revenue per labor hour, which is our critical number." The production reports go into Web's plant-wide information systems and are added into each team's road map every day. "Every day you can watch your invoice dollars go up versus your projection—how close are you, how many work days are left, what's the revenue per man hour average for the team month to date, stuff like that. And those figures are also used to track our bigger numbers, the plantwide numbers, which we have posted on a chalkboard in a little information center."

You couldn't have done all this stuff 20 years ago, which is one reason companies have been slow to develop it. But the information age and open-book management go hand in hand. Well-programmed computers can spit out up-to-the-minute data at virtually no cost. Open-book management shows people what kinds of information they need and how to use the information once they get it. Open-book companies need smart financial people and at least one computer whiz. The combination is unbeatable.

Scoreboards

When it comes to revealing their performance, most companies are the opposite of transparent. They are opaque. The only time anybody has a clue as to how the business is doing is when management issues a pronouncement. You've heard those pronouncements; they're either self-congratulatory or admonishing. When times are good, employees hear: We had a great year. Thanks to everybody for a job well done. Isn't this a great company to work for! When times are bad it's: Sales aren't where they should be. Our costs are too high. We're going to have to cut budgets. Incredibly, managers everywhere expect employees to take these pronouncements at face value, even though people at most companies just shrug them off and go about their business. Unless layoffs are imminent, who really cares how the company is doing? And who believes management, anyway?

Open-book companies, in contrast, tell their people how they're doing every month, every week, even every day. They create *scoreboards* that track the critical numbers and show financial performance.

What's a scoreboard? Sometimes it's little more than a chart or thermometer up on the wall. Maybe it's a handout with an update on the financials, or a report sent out over E-mail. There's no fixed format for a scoreboard; as we'll see, companies mostly create their own and indeed have created an astonishing variety. Companies have also learned some handy rules of thumb for making scoreboarding work—for making it more than an idle exercise in record keeping. Done right, scoreboards are an essential element of creating a transparent company.

Before we get to the nitty-gritty, though, we'd better be clear about the nature of the beast. Plenty of companies these days, though miserly with real how-the-business-is-doing information, *do* put all kinds of charts and graphs up on the wall. The charts show customer-service reps how many calls they've handled today. They tell machine operators how they're doing on quality and output. They track daily shipments, customer complaints, percentage of on-time delivery, and a dozen other measures of performance.

These may be important operational metrics, and open-book companies are as likely as anybody else to include them on their scoreboards. But there are some fundamental differences between open-book scoreboards and conventional charts and graphs—differences that go right to the heart of open-book management.

For one thing, open-book companies understand that *no number exists in isolation*. It may be great for a plant to hit 98 percent on-time delivery—but not if so many people are working overtime and freight expense is so high that the plant is becoming noncompetitive. "The power isn't in the numbers, it's in the relationship between the numbers," says Fred Plummer, a progress coordinator with Amoco Canada. "Let's go back to that example about the oil-well service technicians cutting their vehicle costs. Well, they can do that easily, just by not doing any driving. But that's hardly the point. The point is to reduce vehicle costs while maintaining or even increasing service and production levels. You track all those numbers so that they learn to think about the relationship."

Second, numbers on a scoreboard are powerful only insofar as people *want* to make them move in the right direction. ("You gotta wanna," says Jack Stack in *The Great Game of Business*.) A performance goal chalked up on the board by management with no input from employees and no obvious relation to anything that matters is not a great motivator over the long haul. Managers often fool themselves on this one; people do like to test their skills and do respond to challenges, so they'll often rise to the occasion and beat some arbitrarily imposed target. But people aren't pigeons, either. Unless they see some reason for hitting the targets, performance challenges get old fast.

Third, operational numbers derive their ultimate meaning from their *effect on financial performance*. Financial performance, however an individual company may define it, is a business's goal. Financial success creates wealth and opportunities. It provides job security.

It's the objective that gives meaning and purpose to what people in a company do every day. Operational numbers are no more than a means to that end. A scoreboard that charts only operational numbers is like a basketball scoreboard that records shots taken or rebounds made but doesn't record points.

This point eludes any number of managers, consultants, and business gurus. Measure, they say. Track. All well and good, but let's also measure and track (and communicate) the numbers that really matter, the ones that show not just whether you did a good job today but how your business is doing in the marketplace.

The essential difference between an open-book scoreboard and all those scattered charts and graphs, of course, is that the open-book scoreboard is integrated with the whole management system. It tracks the numbers that a company has determined are critical. It reports the financials. It tracks all these numbers not in the abstract, but against the company's plan. The scoreboard may also show how people are doing toward their bonus, and it may include the kind of essential business information that senior managers take for granted but employees don't always know. (Who are our biggest customers? What was our stock price yesterday? How much did we bid that job for?) The scoreboard is the basic vehicle of communication in an open-book company. It's what ties the disparate elements of open-book management together.

Kinds Of Scoreboards

Companies have come up with all manner of vehicles for getting the word out; many use more than one method. A roundup:

Bulletin boards and information centers. Cascade Bookkeeping, in Portland, Oregon, has a hallway full of whiteboards showing the status of every account and every job, as well as the company's financial statements. The financials include accounts receivable—important in a small business!—and month-to-date billings. The boards are updated daily. At OASIS, a contract furniture installer in Seattle, the board shows not only financial performance but stock value and the company's top 25 or 30 clients. "Everybody's aware of who's really providing us with our dollars," says vice president and co-owner Michael Taylor. Web Industries' Framingham plant has an information center with all the factory's production and financial data posted. S&R Industries, in Baker City, Oregon, has a

40-foot wall displaying financial results, forecasts, the status of individual jobs, and "any other information we want to share with employees," says president Randy Johnson. Are you worried that outsiders will see sensitive financial data? Tom Neilsen of Neilsen Manufacturing Company has a public bulletin board charting key operational measures—and another board with financial data behind his office door, visible only to people who are invited into his office.

Handouts and meetings. Companies often post or hand out paper copies of their scoreboards. Mimi Taylor of Vectra describes the system in her company: "The daily charts are posted. We have an overhead amount, and we know that our sales—actually our throughput or value-added sales—have to be over the daily overhead costs. That chart tracks it." Nothing fancy here; the charts are just 8½ by 11 sheets of paper. "They're distributed to managers and posted all over the building by nine o'clock in the morning. Some managers have them on their doors, some on their department bulletin boards. Our building's very large, so we have to put stuff up wherever people need it to be."

Other companies distribute scorecards at meetings. When you're keeping score, the meetings lend themselves to hoopla and celebration (or commiseration). Commercial Casework asks volunteer teams of employees to cook up a big lunch for the monthly all-company meetings. After lunch, managers report the performance of each department. Foldcraft holds its monthly meetings in a rented church hall. Four overhead projectors display a 15-column income-statement template on a big wall: sales, purchases, throughput, all the way over to after-tax income, with rows for each team or department. As people file in, employees fill in monthly results, opinions for the current month, projections for the end of the year. "Then they'll need to explain the variance, if there is one," says chief financial officer Doug Westra. "Why did the actual come in different from their opinion last month? Usually the operational team leader will do the talking for the group, but anyone from the department can answer."

Charts, graphs, thermometers. Walk into the offices of Amoco Canada in a high-rise building in downtown Calgary, Alberta, and the walls are a riot of color; charts and graphs from the division's many business units track production, expenses, the status of exploration projects, and a dozen other variables. At Crisp Publications, in Menlo Park, California, hand-lettered score sheets show budget and performance figures by month for each department. At Omega Point Laboratories Inc., a fire-testing laboratory in Elmendorf, Texas, the bonus plan is pegged to targets for profit margin and current ratio—and accounting/systems specialist David Robbins has put two thermometers in his office, one for each of the two goals. Visual In-Seitz, a multimedia business-presentation company in Rochester, New York, uses a thermometer that tracks actual sales, contracts, and projected profit. "We fill it in as we go and start another thermometer at the beginning of each month," says chief executive Chad Engler.

Newsletters. Sarah Montgomery, vice president of operations for Woodpro Cabinetry, writes a monthly newsletter called *Profit Watch* that goes out to the company's 90 employees. The one-page, front-and-back sheet summarizes Woodpro's financials and critical numbers and tells employees where they stand on the bonus. It also includes regular features such as "Cost Alert," which highlight potential problems and opportunities. Putman Publishing Company, in Chicago, produces a two-page in-house newsletter every week. Dubbed *Game Day*, it shows key numbers for each of the company's magazines and other business units. A highlight: "Stat of the Week." "Maybe it'll be return on sales," explains Putman's president, John Cappelletti. "Or profit versus goal. Or competitive numbers such as market share, or the critical numbers from auxiliary profit centers such as trade shows and newsletters. It's on the front page, in a chart. So people get to see the results for the different magazines, the results and returns, the successes. And then they know where to go and who to ask, 'Hey, how are you doing that?'"

Electronics. Maybe not surprisingly, companies have created a wide variety of electronic scoreboards.

- Nims Associates, a computer-education consulting firm in Decatur, Illinois, utilizes customized software to link its 210 consultants, most of whom work at clients' locations. The software provides E-mail, electronic bulletin boards, and discussion forums. On the last day of each month, the company posts its operating numbers for employees to review.

- Employees of Wascana Energy, in Regina, Saskatchewan, can call up a host of scoreboards just by clicking on the Performance Management icon on their computer screen. Every department has its own set of goals, explains company treasurer

Steven Reilly, and the computer shows performance-to-plan numbers along with a department's most recent action plan to address variances.

- Sony Display Device San Diego, a California division of the big electronics company, uses a protected World Wide Web site (an *Intranet*) to communicate performance and financial information to 200 employees on one of its production lines. "It has key performance indicators, such as good output quantity, reject costs, and inventory discrepancy, along with full profit-and-loss financials," says Dirk Macfarlane, a financial manager at the facility.

- Visual In-Seitz, which produces projects for individual clients, employs a custom database that tracks people's time and expenses on jobs. Each employee inputs relevant information every day; once a week, the database manager distributes an electronic file containing the consolidated data. "Producers can see what they'll need to bill to make a reasonable profit on the job," explains Chad Engler.

Making Scoreboarding Work
Scoreboards all over!

If you can't use computers, or if most employees don't have easy access to one, make sure that everybody *sees* a board. If your facility is large, that means putting up boards in every department or unit. If your employees are geographically dispersed, it means figuring out some way, paper or electronic, to get the word out. Terminix Company, a pest-control company with six offices in North Carolina, transmits a scoreboard every day to each of its offices. "It prints on the computer system, and they can post it," says president Harden Blackwell.

Establishing a line of sight

Scoreboards track team and department numbers; they also track corporate or business-unit performance. There's a connection here, and people need to know it. A staff department's budget is part of an expense line, and if the department's expenditures run over budget, that line will go up. Defect rates may affect rework numbers and shipments, which will be reflected on the cost-of-goods-sold line.

In larger organizations, of course, the contribution of any one team or department may be small. But it is never zero. People need to keep *their* numbers in control. The scoreboard can help them understand the importance of that control, by showing them how they affect business performance.

Keeping it lively—and up-to-date

Scoreboards don't happen by accident! They have to be established, nurtured, cultivated, and kept up-to-date. Teams of volunteers have to make the boards their own and add material every week or every day. Boards that show progress toward a goal are livelier than boards that don't show the connection. Boards that show people how close they are to earning a bonus attract attention. So do boards that have contests, cartoons, and did-you-know facts. You could do worse than emulate Bonanza Nut & Bolt, a distributor of industrial fasteners in Sparks, Nevada. Says president Jim Annis:

> See, we have boards everywhere, in each of the warehouses, that show us what our daily shipping and bookings are. On one board we have what we call "money-making time." That's the amount of available bonus money that's accumulating during the current quarter, backing out the shareholders' shares and a few other things. Everyone has a formula. So on any given day, at any time, they can plug that number into the formula to get a good idea of what their running bonus is.
>
> We also have what we call our "What's Happening" board. It's just a big bulletin board in the main hallway near the bathrooms. I publish the "Food for Thought," which is just a thought for the day, motivational snippets. Then we'll have a Gary Larson comic strip—*The Far Side*—to attract readers. It also contains the minutes for all of the week's team meetings. It's amazing how often that board is read on a daily basis. And across the hall from that is the "Performance" board. When we have all the new goals, we'll post goals and charts. That's so the groups can see how the others are doing.

Caution! People like to keep score; they don't necessarily like to have score kept *for* them, particularly if they fear they'll be punished for poor performance. So listen to employees. What do they want to track? What do they think are fair measures, and what is a good way of scoring them? And watch for unforeseen consequences. At the Trenton, Illinois, plant of Hexacomb Corporation, production crews didn't like the daily score sheets they were getting; shifts were beginning to compete too much with one another, which meant that one shift was likely to leave tougher jobs for the next shift. At the employees' request, managers changed to a weekly report. That balanced out the daily variation and removed the element of unhealthy competition.

**CHAPTER
SIX**

Teaching Business

Training is hot these days. If you work for a big company—or even for a not-so-big one—you'll have no trouble getting additional training. Sharpen up your job skills! ("Advanced Welding," "Lotus Notes for Beginners," "Techniques of Telephone Marketing.") Cultivate new interpersonal skills! ("Managing the Diverse Workplace," "Basic Team Building," "Learning to Listen.") If you need it, you can relearn basic math or take English as a second language. You can go to in-house classes, attend outside seminars and workshops, even take a course at a local college, with your employer picking up the tab.

What you can't do—not easily, anyway—is learn business. Unless you can scrape up the time and money to go back to school, forget about learning how a company works or how it measures its performance. You can learn how to do your own job better. You can't learn why it might matter if you do.

Isn't this bizarre? After all, we live in a business society. Business leaders are admired. Business schools are thriving. Entrepreneurship is up. Millions of people invest in the stock market and follow business news. On the other hand, not many of us other than MBAs and accountants learn even the basic vocabulary of business. We get *profit* confused with *money in the bank*. We assume that because a company has so many million in *revenues*, it must be able to spring for a raise or a new piece of equipment. (If only "they" weren't so cheap!) Financial illiteracy—which means, make no mistake, an inability to understand the fundamental metrics of any business—is common even among people who should know better. Owners of small companies leave the finances to their accountants. (Just tell me how much money I'm making.) Marketing VPs and plant managers know their operational numbers but throw up their hands when asked to calculate return on investment. Meanwhile, your average customer-service reps or machine technicians would be hard put even to identify, say, gross margin on a P&L—not surprising, since no one ever showed them how.

So employees soldier on, in the dark. Not understanding the financials, they don't know why owners and executives make the decisions they do. They aren't aware of the constraints that their company's financial situation puts on their work. Despite all the job-skills training, despite, in many cases, a lot of fancy technical education, they don't really know how to do their jobs better because they don't understand what will make a difference.

Think about what typically happens when a company's management issues one of its periodic dicta about the importance of controlling costs. Most employees don't understand why costs suddenly need to be controlled. Nor do they know much about what would really be effective. So they have only two choices. They can hope the whole thing will go away. (Most choose this option.) Or they can do their diligent best to turn out lights, use both sides of a sheet of paper, and recycle some old parts in hopes that these well-meaning gestures will somehow make a dime's worth of difference to their company's performance. "We've always told our people to watch their costs," one plant manager muses, "but we've never given them the tools to understand what their costs really are."

This is one more area—a big one—in which open-book companies differ from conventional ones. Open-book companies *do* teach business. They expect that people all over the organization will understand those critical numbers and financial statements—that they'll be able to read the scoreboard. This is no trifling ambition! In most cases the companies are starting from scratch. They have to cope with the math or number phobia that makes so many people think they'll never be able to learn that stuff. How do they do it? As we'll see in this chapter, it's partly through an imaginative set of teaching techniques. A lot of them have actually figured out how to make it fun to learn about business. In the next chapter we'll get to another reason the learning sticks: employees get a chance to practice what they have learned, day in and day out. In open-book management, the best reason of all for learning business is that you're expected to *use* what you know.

Teaching employees to understand business makes your organization truly transparent. It also enables employees to work a whole lot smarter. If you distilled open-book companies' experience with business training into ten lessons, here's what they might look like.

1. "What would you like to know?" is a better opening line than "Here's what you have to know." RTW Inc., a Minneapolis-based company that manages workers' compensation claims, came out with this open-book purpose statement: "To create a company of business-literate owners through education and empowerment to build competitive advantage and growth for RTW." Then the company sent out a survey. "There were only three questions," explains finance-team coach Tina Comstock. "It asked '*What opportunities* would you like to see for business learning at RTW?' '*Where* would you best learn this information? Staff meetings? Team meetings? Brown-bag lunches?' and '*How* would you best learn this information? Written materials? Videos? Overheads?' Of course, we also asked what kind of prizes they'd like. I sent it out over E-mail and got back a phenomenal response."

2. Hold a few classes and see how they go. CFO Brent Youngblood of Crisp Publications in Menlo Park, California, taught basic finance to the company's managers in a series of lunchtime classes. Other employees, peering into the conference room, wondered what was going on, and pretty soon were able to sign up for classes of their own. Foldcraft Company was written up in *Inc.* magazine for a series of in-house classes on creating a chocolate-chip-cookie company. Later, as Foldcraft's business evolved, CFO Doug Westra set up a whole new business-simulation course, this one about a company that manufactures school desks (an enterprise close to Foldcraft's real business).

3. Quizzes, games, and contests start things off with a bang. GT Development, in Seattle, launched its business-education program with a ten-question true-false and multiple-choice quiz; get nine right and you're eligible for a $20 prize. I have to pause for a moment to say a word about GT Development. These are the folks who, when they plunged into OBM, wrote a one-act play to explain their company's bonus system. The quiz announcement had a certain panache, too. "Do you balance your checkbook, or let the bank make all the mistakes? Is the P&L a railroad? Is Cash Flow a country-western singer? If GT were insolvent, would we call the EPA? Just how much do you understand about the basics of business finance?" The quiz itself wasn't too easy. (Sample question: "True or False: Under general accounting principles, accounts receivable are not counted as an asset until actually collected.")

"We got a great response," says OBM project manager Jim Meyerdirk. "We held the drawing publicly and announced the winners. Of course, now every time people see me on the floor they ask when the next contest is." (P.S.: The answer to the question is "false." Receivables are an asset, they just aren't the same as cash.)

Short of ideas for games? Don't be. William Dee Pickens, owner of Pool Covers Inc. in Richmond, California, likes to hang a number on the door between the office and the shop. People have to guess what that number is and how it relates to the business. Pickens: "One of the very first ones I put up was 22.5. I just left it there. Pretty soon people began asking questions. Then at the next weekly meeting I said, 'Okay, everyone has a chance to guess what that number was.' Two people guessed it: the average miles per gallon of our fleet. I gave them each $10." Lawyers Title of Oklahoma City, a title-insurance company, played a guess-the-gross game. In preparation, the company provided people with gross-revenue information for the previous month and for the same month the previous year. Prize for the closest answer: $25.

4. Very small companies can do great business training; all it takes is a little time and a lot of imagination. I think of this as the lesson of Julie Lotesto, who, if she weren't doing what she does, would doubtless make a great teacher.

Lotesto is operations manager of Glavin Security Hardware Specialists, an 18-employee locksmith company in downtown Chicago that was getting into OBM. She and owner Tom Glavin decided that they first wanted to make everybody aware of sales— so they posted their monthly sales goal and told everybody that Lotesto would do the Snoopy dance if they made it.

The Snoopy dance? "We made the goal by $93," explains Lotesto. "Everybody was so excited about it, I had half the company standing around the computer waiting for me to print out the sales number. So then I went out and rented a Snoopy costume. Have you ever watched Charlie Brown? Snoopy does the victory dance when he gets really happy. Well, we found the Snoopy music, and I came downstairs with the balloons tied to my tail, and I did the Snoopy dance in front of the whole company. In the costume.

"After that, everybody watched the numbers and everybody wanted to see what sales were each month. All motivated by my making a fool of myself."

But, hey, this was only the start.

Next, Lotesto got teams of employees to invent mock businesses in security-related industries. She walked them through the start-up process, including figuring out their capital needs and developing a sales and financial plan. Then, over a six-month period, she presented each group with a series of decision-making situations. (Sample: "Your largest customer comes to you with a $35,000 job but says he can't pay you for 60 days. Do you take the work?") The teams had to allocate resources according to what they decided, and then could see the results of their decisions on the income statements and balance sheets Lotesto prepared.

Lotesto then set up formal financial-training classes: a half-hour twice a week, running for several months. She taught them herself. "The balance sheet was the first class. We said, 'List all of your personal assets, everything you own. Now list everything you owe.' It was very basic. We started out the same way with the income statement. 'List all the money that you have coming in. List all the money that you have going out.'" After the basics, she moved on to Glavin's financials—and wound up with a bunch of "A" students. "I now have service technicians with high-school educations who can tell you everything that's in the cost-of-goods-sold line for Glavin. They understand gross margin, gross profit, all the operational expenses, what the operational percentage is, net profit, and net profit before tax."

Training continues as this is written. "Right now we're working on a big push to increase sales. But before we could increase sales, we had to make sure that everyone knew what was involved, what was the cost of sales. Also, twice a week, we pick certain jobs at random and go over the profitability of those jobs. And every Friday morning we go over where our sales are, where's our gross profit, what are our cost of goods, operational expenses, and net profit. We also discuss work-in-process. For our company, work-in-process is a major contributor. We may have an $11,000 job that's taking us two weeks to complete, so the cost of goods goes up. Guys will say, 'If we were to have estimated that job this way, we could have gotten it done quicker.'"

Are Lotesto and Glavin somehow unique? Nope. Deborah Field, accounting manager of Transitions for Health, in Portland,

Oregon, was given the assignment of teaching business literacy to the health-products company's 25 employees. To introduce basic financial terms, she delivered a series of six one-hour lectures called "Numbers Talk (and Tell a Story)." The keys to the success of these classes, she says, were participation, variety, and fun. She created written handouts on financial terms, showed a video explaining the income statement and balance sheet, played a *Jeopardy*-style game to answer company-related business questions, and led small-group problem-solving sessions. "In a relatively short time the employees learned a lot and were much less fearful of numbers."

Field's *pièce de résistance*, developed in conjunction with a local vendor, was a game called The Numbers Drive Me Wild.

It's a big board game, five feet by three feet. A safari theme played in cross-departmental teams. There are eight business activities that teams have to complete over an eight-week period. Everybody got time to do their assignments at work. The teams were guided by the safari leader—me—but were pretty much on their own when it came to completing assignments. The teams moved along the game board through the jungle by rolling dice and landing on different-colored squares. Each color represented a different business activity: a cash transaction, a sale, whatever.

One of the favorites was the Creative Cash activity. And were people ever creative! One team, the Kenya Cash Carnivores, put together a videotape interview of different employees and their relationship to cash in the company. One sales-related assignment was to develop a proposal and break-even analysis for a new product. The Wandering Wildebeests developed Safari Charms necklaces, and actually sold product to employees. They determined they needed to sell 41 to break even on an investment of 200 necklaces.

Every time a team completed one of the eight activities, they received an animal stamp on their passport. To succeed at the game, they had to collect all the animal stamps and either read *Open-Book Management* or present the month's numbers to all the employees. Along the way, people got many small tokens of accomplishment for outstanding individual performance. One exceptional participant got the Big Banana award each week.

All the employees succeeded and were rewarded with a certificate of completion and a celebration with food, drink, and live African drum music performed by Portland's premier musician, Obo Addy.

5. Big companies can do some pretty cool stuff, too (so long as they are equally imaginative). At 600-employee Wascana Energy, an oil-and-gas company headquartered in Regina, Saskatchewan, they came up with their own innovative approach.

First, the company designated a team of employees to figure out exactly what kind of business education employees needed. The team's first conclusion: people should get *industry-specific* training materials. The team then wrote and produced an 86-page workbook—"an icebreaker," says team leader Joan Beisel—that walks readers through oil-and-gas-company financials. Cartoons, a folksy touch, and specific references to Wascana give the book a friendly feel. Before rollout, team members spent a day and a half with representatives from company units. Those reps were responsible for distributing the workbook to employees and for answering questions.

Meanwhile, Wascana financed the development of a computerized business-simulation game, customized for oil and gas, by Great Game Solutions (a Calgary, Alberta, consulting company affiliated with Springfield ReManufacturing Corp.). When the game—dubbed The Great Game of Treasure Hunt—was completed, the business-education team set up a tournament to play it. "We left it up to individuals to form playing teams and then contact a facilitator for an introductory session," says Beisel. Everyone who completed the game during the next few months—about two-thirds of the company's employees did so—was eligible for a $100 prize.

Finally, a series of sessions called W.E. Connect reviewed the business-education lessons, walked employees through Wascana's financials, and showed the links between financial performance and the company's gain-sharing bonuses. Attendance was *very* good; employees couldn't get their gain-sharing checks until they had attended a W.E. Connect session.

With minor variations, this same scenario has been followed by RR Donnelley & Sons Company's Northeastern Division (Lancaster, Pa.; see Chapter 20), Digital Equipment Corporation's semiconductor manufacturing division (Hudson, Mass.), and Amoco Canada (Calgary, Alberta). The computerized simulation games developed for all these companies seem fanciful. Donnelley's, for example, called Celestial Cheese, has players running a mining company on the moon. On second glance, though, they're highly sophisticated and industry specific. That mining company is capital intensive, just like printing. It produces a variety of products to customer specifications, just like printing. Quality control is important, just like printing. And so on. Result: players manage a business very much like their own over a ten-year period, making strategic decisions and tracking their progress on their company's financials. The cost for a large company: about $75 per employee.

6. Make the connection between the financials and what people do on the job. AES Corporation, headquartered in Arlington, Virginia, includes financial education with the many other technical classes that its power-plant operators take. When it gets to the exercises, students do chores such as a net-present-value analysis of that new bulldozer the plant is about to purchase. The Boundless Technologies facility, in Hauppauge, New York, offered employees a series of business-education classes and made a point of linking what people learned to their jobs. "The last thing we added to the class was a session on how their individual jobs impact the different line items," says HR director Steven Green. "They wanted to know, 'Where do I fit into the big picture?'"

Amoco Canada uses what Fred Plummer calls drill-down sheets to explain the link between daily work and the financials. The sheets are nothing more than diagrams of how an employee's job fits in. You, the oil-well service technician, drive a truck. Your truck expenses show up *here*, on the "operations costs" line of your facility's financial report. Your facility's numbers show up *here*, on the income statement of your business unit. Any company can do this, because every employee's job affects some budget, some cost line, some portion of the income statement. All you have to do is graph—and then teach—the connection.

Bonanza Nut & Bolt took Amoco's approach and turned it upside down. President Jim Annis asked his employees to write down ways in which they could affect the bottom line. Good starting point for a business education program.

7. Have fun! Learning doesn't have to be painful. (When it is, people don't learn.) Founder Patrick Kelly took Physician Sales & Service, in Jacksonville, Florida, from start-up to industry leadership in a mere 13 years. One of PSS's secrets: active, involved employees, many of whom have built up substantial nest eggs because of the company's stock-ownership programs. Talk about transparent! Walk into one of the company's many branches and the walls are practically papered with financial reports, sales reports, margin analyses, and so on. Even so, Kelly felt that too many employees' eyes were glazing over during the monthly meetings to review branch P&Ls. "He told me, figure out some way to make this stuff *fun*," remembers corporate trainer Susan Parker.

So Parker hired some outside help and came up with The PSS Challenge. Once a month, every branch's employees go off-site— to an amusement park, bowling alley, miniature-golf arcade (a *putt-putt*, if you live in the South)—and play a game modeled on the TV show *Family Feud*. It gets pretty raucous. Team members yell out the answers to business questions, put their heads together to figure out the toughies ("Name a component of selling expense"), and pile up points toward prizes such as jackets and watches. Every month's game focuses on a different topic: the balance sheet, purchasing and inventory, customer service. Teams prepare for the game by studying hint sheets posted back at the office.

Grand Circle Corporation, an adventure-travel company in Boston, kicked off its business education with a gala off-site retreat in the summer, complete with skits. CEO Alan Lewis devised the structure:

First, Grand Circle divided its 200-plus employees (at the time; the company just keeps growing) into 19 teams. Each team was assigned a specific product, such as a tour of Greece or a Caribbean cruise. The mission: come up with recommendations to improve the quality and profitability of the product. Teams got their assignments three weeks before the company's annual outing. That gave them time for preliminary research, such as learning how Grand Circle produced its product P&Ls and how it measured quality (e.g., the number of travelers who rate a tour "excellent").

At the outing itself—a daylong event dubbed "BusinessWorks '95"—in-house teachers assigned to each team led exercises that taught employees more about both generic and product-specific P&Ls. Then the teams brainstormed. How could the product be made better and more profitable? Maybe the pace should be slower, so travelers wouldn't get too tired. Maybe the pretrip cancellation rate—an important element of profitability—could be lowered. Next, each team performed a short skit presenting its key recommendations. The top three presenters received cash prizes ranging from $250 to $1,000.

After the outing, teams wrote up their recommendations, backed by appropriate numbers. Each then met with Lewis and the managers responsible for its product. The managers had to respond to the teams in writing, explaining what was being done with each recommendation and why. One recommendation aimed at lowering a particular tour's cancellation rates by two percentage points had an immediate payoff; the company figured it would increase sales by $31,000. But Lewis felt the real payoff would be over the longer term, as associates came to understand how Grand Circle Travel makes its money.

8. There are a lot of good tools available. PSS and Grand Circle designed their own games; Wascana and the others commissioned custom computerized business simulations. If you've got the money and resources, great. If you don't, there are plenty of materials on the market right now.

> *Board games* include Profit & Cash, Zodiak, Apples and Oranges, and Enterprise Profitability. (These names are all registered trademarks of the game manufacturers.) Schrock Cabinet Company—a unit of AB Electrolux located in Dublin, Ohio—played Profit & Cash with 40 managers. In the game, teams roll dice and move chips to squares that demand an action (make a sale, pay an expense, collect a receivable). Then they fill out wall-size scorecards recording sales, inventory, expenses, and so forth. Schrock's HR director, Mark Stewart, was pleased with the results: "People came away with a much better feel for the intricacies of making money." Tip: If you can, organize players into a tournament, the way Wascana did with its computer-simulation game. Everybody plays. Winners get prizes. An Intel facility did that with Profit & Cash and found that even its busy engineers were making time to play (not to mention watching their team's progress on the tournament chart).

> *Workshops and seminars* include The Accounting Game, The Financial Game for Decision-Making (both offered by Educational Discoveries Inc., in Boulder, Colo.), and a host of more specialized offerings—some, for example, aimed primarily at companies with employee stock ownership plans. Trainers can come into your company. Or you can send employees to public seminars. The Wellbridge Company, a Boston-area

health-and-fitness-center concern, sent 30 managers to The Accounting Game. Several large companies have hired The Accounting Game's producers to do specially tailored versions in-house.

Workbooks in basic finance are available from publishers such as Crisp Publications, in Menlo Park, California. *The Yo Yo Company*, produced by Springfield ReManufacturing Corporation's BizLit division, is a favorite among open-book companies. It takes readers through the creation of a simple manufacturing company (yes, yo-yos) and shows how to create simple financials. It's also available in an interactive version on disk.

Books take a long time to produce, and the list of available resources will doubtless have changed by the time you read this. So get in touch with me (see the Resources page at the back of the book), or contact some open-book companies themselves and find out what they're using. Generic instructional software in particular is scarce as this is written; the interactive Yo Yo disk is one of a small number of programs available. That will change as more and more companies get interested in teaching business.

9. There's nothing like on-the-job training. "Most of our education came as people worked on budgets!" says Ken McBride of Lawyers Title of Oklahoma City. It isn't so different at the best-known open-book company of all, Springfield ReManufacturing Corporation. SRC does little in the way of formal financial education. It simply expects employees to get whatever help they need and familiarize themselves with the relevant financials so they can take part in budgeting, planning, and discussions about group performance. The next section tells how to build this expectation into people's job descriptions.

10. Experiment! A bunch of open-book companies got started on business education by making a big blowup of a dollar bill—the sales dollar—and showing people where it all went, by dime and nickel and penny. Frank Topinka, president of McKenna Professional Imaging, in Waterloo, Iowa, likes to ask financial questions at company meetings—and pass out a few bucks for correct answers. Mike Rydin of Heavy Construction Systems Specialists, a Houston software company, gave employees a pool of about $5,000 in company money to invest in the stock market. People voted on which stocks to buy, which meant that everyone had to bone up on matters such as price-to-earnings ratios. At Bagel Works, a New Hampshire–based chain, employees have to take and pass a quiz on the income statement before they can get their bonuses. Braas Company, an Eden Prairie, Minnesota, distributor, provides in-house finance classes, but they're taught by nonfinancial people. ("I'm an accountant," scoffs assistant controller Doreen Eng. "For me to teach accounting would be ludicrous!") Web Industries' Framingham plant periodically asks frontline workers to lead reviews and discussions of the monthly financials. ("They sit down with our accountant the day before the meeting and go over the P&L in detail," says organizational development director Hugh McGill.)

It's easy to do business education wrong. One CEO confessed to me that he had sat his employees down for three hours one afternoon and delivered a nonstop lecture on the company's financials that left their heads spinning. "It was way too much," he sighed. Short of that, there are any number of possible pitfalls. Classes and explanations can be too complex or too simple for the intended audience. Games can misfire. But the biggest mistake you can make is to do business education in a vacuum, before people have any idea why it might be worthwhile to learn what all those numbers mean. Business training is part of the whole structure of open-book management; without that structure, it's just another chore foisted off on employees by the folks in charge, and it will get the response it deserves.

Second Principle:
A Company of
Businesspeople

Overview: On Empowerment and Other Buzzwords

The *goal* of creating a transparent company is to enable people to get the work done more effectively and thereby to boost the organization's business performance. What does it mean to get the work done more effectively? Well, in part it means learning to make smarter decisions. And in part it means learning to take responsibility for the impact of your work.

Frontline employees make a zillion decisions every day in doing their jobs. Warehouse workers decide to pick and ship this part rather than that one (but is it the right part or not?). Store clerks decide whether to go out of their way to help a customer find that blue sweater in medium. Hotel cleaning staff decide whether rooms and hallways are clean enough, while front-desk clerks decide how to handle a guest's complaint about a troublesome TV. The higher up the occupational ladder you go, the more decisions employees make. Nurses, computer programmers, and customer-service reps can't do their jobs without making hundreds of significant decisions every day.

Of course, there are standards and procedures and rules for all these tasks and occupations, presumably so that employees will make the *right* decisions. But standards, procedures, and rules have to be spelled out and taught. They also have to be enforced.

For a while, the industrial engineers thought they could manage this. They analyzed jobs and timed factory workers' motions. They wrote down exactly how many parts could be machined in an hour and exactly what workers should do to meet that standard. (Later, those standards would be incorporated into union contracts.) They hired foremen and supervisors, who trained their employees, then alternately threatened and cajoled them into working up to standard. Over time, the industrial model spilled over into offices: so many calls handled, so many forms processed, so many customers waited on every hour.

These standards haven't disappeared. Salaried lawyers and consultants have to bill a certain number of hours; truck drivers must cover a certain number of miles. Directory-assistance operators—those who haven't yet been automated out of a job—typically get only a few seconds to handle an inquiry.

But it has been getting harder and harder for companies to set and enforce effective standards. Technology has eliminated a lot of unskilled (read "easily supervised") tasks. Cost pressures have forced companies to get rid of supervisors. More and more people work in service businesses; they're on the phone, or on the road with customers. The result of all these trends is that employees have to make more decisions—and can't always rely on standards and rules, or on a supervisor's judgment. Is the cable installer supposed to handle twelve customers a day even if one difficult job takes three hours? Should the machine operator interrupt production now because the statistical-process-control charts show that part sizes are creeping up toward tolerance limits?

In short, companies can't "boss it in" any more. They can't simply take a random group of people (who may or may not give a damn about the business), tell them *exactly* what to do, and then watch like a hawk to make sure they do it right.

Smart companies know this—which is why the concept of *empowerment*, in both its old and its new guises, has gained such currency in the past decade.

For a while, the move toward empowering employees was cautious and circumscribed. Companies asked some of their employees to make some of those decisions about their work themselves, without direct supervision. They put people on teams and gave the teams responsibility for clearly delineated matters such as scheduling. *Self-managing teams* and *participative management* were the buzzwords of the day.

In the 1990s, all hell broke loose on the empowerment front. Managers who wanted to be on the cutting edge, said the gurus, had to forget about reengineering and start *dee*ngineering. They were supposed to dismantle structures and hierarchies and lines of authority and let people come together spontaneously to solve problems. The new model of the plant or office was no longer the well-oiled machine; it was the biological organism, which adapts and evolves in its struggle to survive. People would come together to solve problems. They would form groups, take on whatever needed to be done, then let the groups dissolve. ("We function like an amoeba that flows with the environment and constantly reshapes its body," one company owner gushed to a newspaper columnist.) The new buzzwords were phrases such as *self-organization* and *bottom-up leadership.*

It was easy to get carried away. Management theorists wrote recklessly about creating chaos, about allowing "unforeseen problem-solving mechanisms" to emerge. Working managers could be forgiven for wondering how, exactly, they were supposed to do away with those oppressive corporate structures, and what, exactly, those unforeseen mechanisms might be. Still, there was more than a grain of truth behind this just-do-it style of empowerment, and it lay in the obsolescence of traditional command-and-control techniques. If you can't lay down and enforce standards, after all, you *have* to let standards emerge—and you have to suppose (or hope) that people will find ways of accomplishing the objectives that they set for themselves.

The real trouble with the whole movement toward empowerment wasn't the occasional rhetorical excess. Excess is inevitable in a time of rapid change. It was that the gurus (and many of the experimenters) saw empowerment in isolation from the business of the company. Great: employees would set goals by themselves and figure out on their own how to meet the standards. But how would they know whether what they were doing fit in with what everybody else in the organization was doing? Or whether it fit in with where the company was headed? How would people *learn* to make decisions that furthered the company's business objectives rather than decisions that somehow worked at cross purposes? And by what standards would people be held accountable for their decisions? You can talk about abolishing structure all you want, but in a business, someone is necessarily responsible for the business's performance. And that someone can't very well say, "Gee, I don't know what's happening in the organization—people are out solving problems on their own."

Open-book companies take a more integrated approach toward empowerment.

They understand, first, that *empowerment occurs within a structure.* Structures in a company may need to be changed (or circumvented) from time to time. They may need to be made more fluid or more flexible. But there is no such thing as an organization without a structure. Structure ensures that everyone pulls in the same general direction.

They also understand that *empowerment is a learning process.* It does no good to put people on a team and give them responsibility for scheduling, say, if they don't know how scheduling affects their organization's output and business performance. People need the information that will guide their decisions, and they need to be able to understand it. If the organization isn't transparent—if people don't understand the business and *see the business effects* of their decisions—empowerment is a sham.

Finally, they understand that *empowerment is ultimately a system of mutual accountability.* You are responsible for your group's *performance*, which means you are responsible for your group's *decisions*. (And the "you" in that sentence doesn't mean only the manager in charge of the group, it means everybody.)

Employees in a conventional company, one that works according to old lay-down-the-standards principles, naturally see themselves as hired hands. Their job is to do whatever the boss says (or whatever is spelled out in the union contract). Companies that empower their employees want them to go beyond this definition of the job; they want people to use their heads, to solve problems, to make smart decisions. Open-book companies take the next logical step, which is to teach (and expect) employees to think and act like businesspeople. They expect them to understand and help shape the company's business objectives, then to take responsibility for their part in furthering those objectives.

How to do it? The open-bookers have developed some simple first steps—steps that encourage learning—and some sophisticated systems and procedures for ensuring accountability. The next two chapters will examine their evolving practice of empowerment— *real* empowerment.

First Steps: Learning to Take Responsibility

Maybe you read the article in the *Wall Street Journal*. It was about a power plant in Uncasville, Connecticut, built and operated by AES Corporation.*

AES, headquartered in Arlington, Virginia, is one of the bright lights of the young independent power generation industry. The company was founded in 1981 by Roger W. Sant and Dennis W. Bakke, both of whom had worked for the Federal Energy Administration. By 1996 it was operating 26 plants in nine countries, with another 8 under construction. Its revenues were $835 million. Its stock was listed on the New York Stock Exchange.

But it was, well, an *unusual* company. It did things like sponsor the planting of millions of trees in Central America to help offset the carbon dioxide emissions from its power plants. It built schools in Oklahoma, near one of its plants, and in Pakistan, near another, and donated them to the community. The prospectus announcing the company's initial public offering of stock in 1991 explained that "an important element of AES is its commitment to four major 'shared' values: to act with integrity, to be fair, to have fun, and to be socially responsible" and warned that "if the Company perceives a conflict between these values and profits, the Company will try to adhere to its values."

What had caught the eye of the *Journal*'s reporter, however, wasn't so much the external good works as the way the business seemed to operate internally. In particular, he focused on what was known as the cash-investments task force.

---

*"Making Sure Work is 'Fun'," by Alex Markels. July 3, 1995; p.1.

The Connecticut plant—known as AES Thames, after the river on which it was situated—maintained a debt-reserve fund of about $35 million, as required by its loan covenants. This money had to be invested in CDs, short-term commercial paper, and other high-grade debt instruments. In most companies this would be the responsibility of the CFO or the CFO's staff. At AES Thames it was the responsibility of a volunteer group of plant technicians—blue-collar employees. They investigated interest rates. They placed the buy-and-sell calls to brokers each week. They made the decisions.

I figured I'd better visit this place, and one cold day in January I did just that. I talked with Dan Rothaupt, the plant manager, and had lunch with people who worked there. One of these people, a control-room technician named Greg Russell, took me on a tour. The reality of the place was even more surprising than I had expected.

Take that cash-investments task force, for example. I figured that would be the plant's new-management showpiece, the one thing everybody wanted to talk about. Nope. It just wasn't that big a deal. "Oh, yeah, I did that," said Russell. "I was a little nervous at first. But we knew we had so much to invest by a certain time, and we made the calls. It was a lot of fun." The people who did the investing, explained Rothaupt, had undergone the plant's basic training course in finance and could call on him or the plant's accountant for help if they needed it. Mostly, they didn't. "They do the calling. They're responsible for it. And they learn things! It wouldn't be unusual for the people on this task force to know which way interest rates are going, when's the date of the next Fed meeting, what's the latest unemployment rate, and so on."

At any rate, that task force was just one of many. Another task force was in the process of interviewing health insurers. Another was charged with overseeing annual reviews, and still another with planning periodic celebrations for all the employees. A dozen or so task forces contributed to the preparation of the budget. "We'll look at efficiency, operations, maintenance, and so on," explained James Luckey, a materials-handling superintendent. "We'll go out and make phone calls. How much is insurance going to be? How much repair material are we likely to need? When we come up with the budget, the task forces present it to Dan and the CEO."

AES Thames was—is—a transparent organization. Reports on power production and other variables are posted daily. The complete financials are shared with everybody at monthly meetings. Most AES people have taken the financial course, which teaches concepts such as internal rate of return and earnings per share and how to figure depreciation on a capital investment. As a result, empowerment can be built right into the culture of the place. AES Thames has no shift supervisors and very little administrative staff. People do things themselves. Mechanics and shift operators, for example, order replacement parts, ensuring a minimum of downtime. "There was a failure on the limestone crusher the other day," said James Luckey. "The part we needed cost about $500, and we could get it over the weekend for an extra $100. Looking at the economics of the limestone operation, we figured it would be cheaper to spend the money and get it airmailed.

"So we just did it. The technicians did it."

Getting Started

You want a company in which your employees can take on that kind of responsibility and can be trusted to make smart decisions? Here are some first steps.

Delegate responsibility for little things. Every business has a few nagging little problems, things that no one is quite on top of or that never seem to get fixed. Figure out how to get employees involved in fixing them and then tracking them to make sure they stay fixed.

Bay State Press, in Framingham, Massachusetts, calls its trouble spots loss centers. "You know what they are," says controller Fred Saul, "the bottlenecks, the problem areas, the sinkholes for time and money." Saul decided to take them to the company's ten-member employee advisory board, which was set up to help management and employees communicate their concerns to one another. One loss center at the company: all the unpaid work required to clean up customers' electronic files in the prepress department before a job could be prepared for printing. Following the advisory board's discussion of the issue, one employee devised a prepress checklist to identify possible problems—and Bay State Press revised its prepress procedures so that customers could be billed for extra work when appropriate. "We expect this to save the company a *lot* of money," says Saul.

Jim's Formal Wear, headquartered in Trenton, Illinois, is a tuxedo wholesaler with seven regional centers. The whole company was working to improve its quality, which was measured by the number of times a customer's order was incorrectly filled and had to be replaced. The center in Seguin, Texas, kept having quality problems, though—until the employees at that center decided to establish what they called the "extra eyeball board." Operations vice president Dale Hoffmann explains the idea:

> It's just a big dry-erase board that sits in the common area. What they decided was, any account needing a replacement that's our fault more than one week in a row would go on the board. Everybody gets a printout of those accounts, too, so they know who they are. When those orders come through the department, they do a double check to make sure that the order's okay.
>
> Then, in customer service, those accounts are put on the "nurturing list." The customers get "oops" cards that say we're sorry, we're trying to do our best. When they order again they get a thank-you card. And we call them: "Did you receive the order? Was everything okay?" Results have been terrific. People on that nurturing list wind up becoming *better* customers. And so, from that experience, one of the centers thought it would be a cool idea to send customers a birthday card on the anniversary date of their becoming an account of ours. So we printed up happy-birthday cards: "We just wanted to recognize your anniversary with us." We send cards out to the plant, so that everyone can sign them. It's a low-cost way to boost customer relations.

In some companies, people learn to take responsibility for fixing everyday problems just by getting together regularly to go over the week's work. Visual In-Seitz, a Rochester, New York company that prepares business presentations for corporate clients, has a nice little wrinkle on this common practice: they hold the weekly meetings in a nearby bar.

CEO Charles (Chad) Engler chuckles as he describes it: "Okay, this may sound a little odd. But every Thursday afternoon at 3:30, the 24 production people and I go off-site to a local bar, have a few beers, and discuss what's going on. We take the first hour or so just to talk, maybe about problems we're seeing or possible solutions. Often we break down into smaller groups to tackle specific issues." Production problems are resolved at this meeting; sales problems at a separate meeting of the company's 6 salespeople.

Create suggestion systems, open-book style. Most companies' suggestion systems are window dressing; employees don't use them, and managers don't respond if they do. An open-book suggestion system can be different, because suggestions are informed by a knowledge of the business.

Here's the way the system works at Pettit Fine Furniture, a manufacturing company in Sarasota, Florida. The very first day a new employee is hired, he or she gets a bunch of suggestion forms, with a blank space for the suggestion and a checklist for what the idea is expected to accomplish ("My suggestion will: ___Reduce Direct Labor; ____ Save Material; ____ Increase Capacity"; etc.). "The most powerful thing we give them that very first day is a bunch of empty suggestion forms," says company president Kim Kenyon.

> The new employee's team leader and I will sit down and explain the forms and why they're used. People are encouraged to make *any* suggestion. How can we improve quality? How can we lower costs? How can people learn new skills? How can we improve safety?
>
> We tell them, "If you take the time to fill out this form, we guarantee it'll be dealt with." It gets a number and goes on a list, and it has to be dealt with. First they bring it to their weekly team meetings. The team members can say if they think it's a great idea, or they can suggest ways to modify it. But if the whole team vetoes the idea, that person can still present it at the monthly meeting. Then the form comes with a notation: who bought the idea, who didn't, and why. When the team leader and I are introducing the form to a new employee, we flip the page and show them the list of suggestions year-to-date that are still open.

Kenyon, co-owner Bill Pettit, and other managers may or may not make a decision on a team's suggestion; sometimes they'll kick it back to the team involved with notations or suggestions of their own. ("Y'all need to consider the office team's stand on this and how it affects them. Work it out.") One suggestion that proved particularly powerful was varying work schedules. Teams came up with three possible schedules, and people were allowed to choose the schedule that was best for them. "Some people work nine-hour days and then a half-day Friday," says Kenyon. "Others have an hour at lunch instead of a half hour to go home or do errands. So now we have this selling point for new employees."

How many such suggestions in conventional companies have foundered because the work wasn't getting done? In an open-book company, people see instantly if the suggestion cuts into business performance—and have an interest in seeing that it does not.

You want a new piece of equipment? Justify it. Every company hears it: "When are they *ever* going to get us a new . . . ?" And it doesn't matter whether you finish the sentence with "machining center," "office copier," or "delivery truck." But at Boston Laser Plus, a Shrewsbury, Massachusetts, remanufacturer of toner cartridges for laser printers, employees who want new equipment fill out a nine-question form to explain and justify the investment. The questions run from "What are we trying to improve?" and "What are our proposed actions?" all the way through "What is the cost of this change?" and "Does this change fit within our parameters? (budget, space, time, personnel, etc.)" The 14-employee company decided to buy a $10,000 filling machine on the basis of the form. "Once we ran it through all the steps, it turned out to be a no-brainer," says president Dean Heusel.

It isn't so different at IPT Corporation, a Palo Alto, California, company that specializes in outsource product development. President Steve Carr issued a memo that challenged employees to come up with full investment proposals. "Want to spend money?" the memo asked. "Make the case for the bottom line."

Carr's one-page memo explained how to add up the cost of an expenditure—out-of-pocket expense, staff time, and so forth—and how to calculate the payback and estimate its accrual rate. Within a month, people were giving him cost-benefit analyses of proposed new purchases. An office employee calculated how many more mailers could be sent out using a new stuffing machine, and argued that one new client from the mailings would cover the entire cost. An engineer made the business case for a $5,000 software package used in circuit-board design. "The savings, adjusted for burden, justify the cost in as few as two boards," wrote the engineer.

"This is a way of teaching people that it isn't just a matter of raising sales and lowering costs—that along the line you have to spend more to make more profit," says Carr. "It's really about helping them get educated about how and why we make purchases."

Task forces and committees

Plenty of open-book companies follow AES's lead and ask people to join groups charged with a variety of business tasks. The engineers and support staff at Smith & Company Engineers, in Poplar Bluff, Missouri, serve on committees responsible for matters such as updating the company's computer system and studying ideas for business diversification. Sharpsville Quality Products—a company formed when union workers sat in for 42 days to prevent the shutdown of their foundry, then eventually bought it out—formed a Profitability Improvement Committee. (President Jeff Swogger: "The committee has a broad base of people from the shop. To start, we're looking at taking four major areas that we can reduce our cost in: raw materials, scrap, our process materials, and our workers compensation.") S&R Industries, a heavy-steel fabricator in Baker City, Oregon, has a committee of people who oversee the suggestion system. "They run it," says company president Randy Johnson. "They approve or disapprove the suggestions, unless it's a huge dollar item. They come and tell me at the end of the month what was approved and what price they got."

Ultimately, though, what you want isn't just for employees to take responsibility for little things but for them to take responsibility for big things—like budgeting.

Bottom-Up Budgeting (and Planning)

It may be that nothing generates as much fear and loathing in the business world as budgets and the budgeting process. Every year, department heads and middle managers struggle to crunch the numbers, doing their best to justify a few extra people or a new piece of equipment, hoping to tuck some slack into a few little-scrutinized line items. And every year senior executives seem to insist that budgets be pared, even slashed—except, of course, for the occasional year when they decide to pour resources into something, leaving the bewildered manager wondering how to spend the money as fast as everyone seems to want to. Employees, meanwhile, go about their jobs, conscious of a sort of alien being that rules their work lives ("Sorry, the budget won't allow that") and leaves their bosses with a permanently harried look.

Is there an alternative? In open-book companies, the budget is no more than what it was always supposed to be: a tool to make the financials turn out the way they're supposed to. People throughout the organization learn to take responsibility for their budgets. They also learn to understand the connection between meeting the budget, on the one hand, and the company's or business unit's financial performance, on the other. That "line of sight," as John P. Schuster and his colleagues put it, is essential; it reminds everyone that what ultimately matters isn't the performance of any one department but the performance of the whole business.* When the connection is obscured—and when managers are rewarded not on the basis of financial performance but on how big their budget is and whether they meet it or not—it's no wonder that budgeting becomes an exercise in gaming the company.

Starting point: The annual plan

Where do budgets come from? In most organizations, the answer is simple: last year. The managers responsible for budgeting take the old numbers and add as much as they think they can get away with—or cut as much as they're ordered to. In open-book companies, the starting point is the annual plan for the company or business unit as a whole. The plan utilizes last year's numbers only insofar as they affect the organization's goals for the current year (see Chapter 3). Those goals, in turn, set the parameters for budgets. If people understand the goals—and how a budget contributes to them—then suddenly the budget makes sense in a way it never did before.

Historical data are invaluable in preparing a budget, of course. You have to know how much it cost you in the past to deliver a certain volume of sales or a certain service. But to let historical data be the starting point is to turn the whole planning process on its head.

The budgeting process

Preparing a budget is a tremendously important process for an organization: it translates the goals into workaday numbers. How many people do we really need to do our share in realizing the company's objectives? How much support do those people need? What will overhead expenses be? What about materials and outside services? Where can we save some money? Yet, preparing the budget is typically the responsibility of one person, the manager.

---

* *The Power of Open-Book Management* (New York: John Wiley & Sons, 1996), 52ff.

Open-book companies involve as many people as they possibly can. They assign line items to individuals or to task forces. They ask work teams and small departments to get together as a group to research and prepare their own budgets. They hold budgeting sessions to make sure everybody understands the parameters. "We want to get as many thumbprints of ownership on every budget line item as possible," says Tom Neilsen, owner of 170-employee Neilsen Manufacturing, "so we included about 40 people in the process—everyone who has an investment in a line item, or can impact what that number needs to be. First we gave them a whole lot of historical information about what each of those [budget] accounts had been before. Then we had discussion groups in which they talked through issues to anticipate the year coming up. We got down to the level of trying to anticipate maintenance labor, which is real hard to do! But it's being proactive."

At Cascade Bookkeeping, says co-owner Bill Friedman, "We're going off-site to do our annual budget. We had been trying to fit the budgeting into our regular meetings, but there just isn't time. The first part of the process is to assign people to particular line items. There are two teams, and so each is responsible for a little less than half the budget. (I have responsibility for some line items.) The teams designate people to take responsibility for certain items. We'll give them a month to let them look back at what was happening last year. They'll do the research, talk to each other, then put together a preliminary budget. And there's a list of *whys*: 'Here's why this will happen. Here's why this should increase.'"

Mid-States Technical provides its employees with a budget work sheet for every item, coded by division, item, and account number. The work sheet asks the budgeter to list every item that goes into the line, to project costs by month, and to add notes explaining anything that needs to be explained ("mass mailings planned for February and October"). Lawyers Title of Oklahoma City asked its employees to get involved in developing budgets and provided them with help getting started. "We assigned expense categories to people, and people sort of educated themselves and then gave a report at an all-employee meeting. But we also had a person in our accounting department sit down with them in the budgeting process," says Ken McBride. "After several meetings they began to get a better feel for things."

Can larger companies and business units expect every employee to have a hand in the unit's budget? Maybe not—but people can get together as groups to discuss their team's or department's budget and can send representatives to unitwide budgeting meetings. The more thumbprints of ownership there are, the less the budget is an alien being, and the more it becomes a tool that people understand and use.

Thinking Like Businesspeople

Establishing the budget through this kind of process has a salutary effect: suddenly people begin to see themselves as *in business*. Their job is to make their numbers—to do the work they have agreed to do without exceeding their budget (saving any money they can along the way). If the budget needs to be changed during the year, they should understand why and should be able to make a persuasive business case to the company for additional investment. Meanwhile, so long as they stay within their budget, groups should have wide latitude to spend money as they see fit.

This pushes decision making outward, away from the managers and executives, yet ensures that everyone's still heading in the same direction. At Mid-States Technical, employees from each division and department prepare their budgets in line with the company's strategic plan; all the CEO has to do is approve them. During the year, the groups can reallocate items within their budgets if they need to. They can also negotiate trade-offs and reallocations with other parts of the company.

This process also leads people to think about their situation in a new light. If people in a department or a division are running their own little business, then they have "customers"—whoever utilizes their products or services—and "suppliers," whose products or services they require. These customers and suppliers may be internal to the organization, external, or both. They also have an "investor," that is, whatever level of the organization ultimately decides whether or not to support them. Dealing with customers, suppliers, and investors is fundamentally different from dealing with a boss or a bunch of coworkers who happen to work in another department. Nobody tells anybody else what to do; people do things because there's a good business reason for doing them. They also understand that, if there isn't a good business reason for what they want to do, they may not have a job.

At Amoco Canada, the people in the human resources department underwent just this kind of transformation. HR in the past had been a pretty typical staff department; most of its budget went for personnel, and nobody really had much of an idea whether it was operating efficiently. But when Amoco Canada launched open-book management, the HR department launched its own business-education process and began analyzing its activities as if it were a company. Staff members identified HR's outputs, such as benefits administration and personnel record keeping. They analyzed the cost of each output and the fully loaded hourly cost of each person on the staff. They surveyed their "customers"—the operating departments of Amoco Canada—and got feedback on their performance. They brainstormed ways of increasing the value delivered to their customers without increasing costs. When Amoco Canada went through a round of layoffs, HR wasn't spared; it took its cuts along with everybody else. But because the staff knew what it did and how much its activities cost, it could plan how best to continue delivering value—exactly as a business would if faced with a slump in the market.

Being in business isn't easy. But all the people who work for a company are in business, whether they know it or not. The question is whether people *view* themselves as businesspeople, who know why things happen and what they might be able to do about them, or as hired hands, who are victims of events they don't understand.

CHAPTER NINE

Continuous Empowerment

Empowerment—real empowerment—means more than taking responsibility for specific tasks. It means taking responsibility for the work of your team or department. It means taking responsibility for *making your numbers.*

In most companies, this is a manager's job. At least it's supposed to be.

In fact, managers' responsibilities vary all over the map. Ever been in the office of a manager who has one of those little fire hats on his or her desk? Most managers devote enormous amounts of time to putting out fires, solving problems, negotiating disagreements, and filling in for absent or not-yet-hired employees. They also spend hours each week doing paperwork, sitting in meetings, and handling calls from customers—all of which may or may not be essential to their primary task. Their primary task, really, is to see that the department or plant or unit does what it's supposed to do—and does it better, faster, or cheaper than it did it yesterday and last year. Their primary task is to contribute to the company's performance by bringing together people and resources in the most effective way possible. Making the numbers (or bettering them) means simply that a manager is succeeding in that primary task.

But even managers who are able to focus on this task—the lucky ones!—have a challenging job. They have to know what's likely to come down the pike in the coming week and coming months. They have to understand the numbers that measure their unit's performance, so that they can spot unexpected variances and make adjustments as appropriate. They have to think about how to avoid potential bottlenecks. They have to know when to spend money and what to spend it on. Meanwhile, of course, they have to be sure that their people are working hard, doing what they're supposed to do, getting the job done.

Open-book management doesn't abolish a manager's job. But it changes it, sometimes drastically.

In an open-book company, that day-in, day-out responsibility for making the numbers is no longer on the shoulders of one person. It's on the shoulders of an entire group. People in the group learn to watch and understand those numbers, to spot variances, to think of adjustments. They learn to forecast, so that they know what they'll have to do in the future. They think about when and where to spend money—and they keep a watchful eye on the budget so they know what's affordable and what's not. They keep *each other* working hard and focused on the task at hand.

What's left for the manager to do? Plenty. People don't learn those skills by themselves, so managers have to act as coaches and teachers. Employees may not have the experience to make good decisions all the time, so managers have to act as leaders, stepping in when necessary to keep people on track and helping them learn from mistakes. Most important, managers can finally do what they always knew they should be doing but never had time for: think about longer-term, bigger-picture issues; reengineer an operation; investigate some new technology; get out to meet with customers.

In small enough business units, this kind of bottom-up decision making can be built right into the unit's day-to-day operations. Employees can take a hand in developing the annual plan and the budget. They can review their performance and give their forecasts at weekly, all-employee meetings. If the manager lets them, they can solve problems on the spot. That's essentially how Chick-fil-A store owners Joe Clark and Jim Brown have taught their employees to operate. "We used to be in the stores all the time," says Clark. "We were very task-oriented. We'd tell people, 'Wash the dishes.'" Now employees have learned how to budget and to take responsibility for individual line items. They track a simplified P&L weekly. Bit by bit, the stores' young employees have learned to make decisions. "They're involved in marketing, outside sales, even decisions about whether to fix a machine themselves or call a repairman," says Brown. "They'll rearrange shifts if they see a way we can save some money. Our goal is that people should be able to run the business without a supervisor there."

Once you get beyond the smallest scale, however, you need a structure for this kind of bottom-up decision making—a structure that ensures that people are in communication with other departments, that they understand, and can take joint responsibility for, not only their own department's performance but the performance of the whole company or business unit. Springfield ReManufacturing Corporation has developed a model for such a structure of accountability, and open-book companies of all sizes have found that it's adaptable to a wide variety of contexts.

SRC's Huddle System

You haven't read a whole lot about Springfield ReManufacturing Corporation in this book, and you won't, even though it has been a model and inspiration for open-book companies all over the United States. (And not only in the United States; for example, the 55,000-employee ZCCM copper operation in Zambia actually hired consultants affiliated with SRC and taught its methods in several divisions.) SRC's systems are described in detail in *The Great Game of Business*, by Jack Stack with Bo Burlingham, a book that every would-be open-book manager should promptly acquire and read.* Right now, however, I have to tell a little about how SRC operates, because one of its management inventions has been adopted (and adapted) by all kinds of open-book companies. It may be the best systematic way of ensuring the kind of mutual accountability and empowerment that I've been describing.

The SRC story—the buyout of a division from what was then International Harvester and the turnaround subsequently engineered by Jack Stack and his colleagues—first came to light in 1986. Stack had attended a panel discussion on executive compensation sponsored by *Inc.* magazine, and there he shared some of his experiences with the magazine's editors. Intrigued, the editors sent a young reporter named Patricia Amend to visit SRC. She returned with a wealth of interesting material, including the fact that SRC used the idea of games to explain business to its employees. The editors then dispatched a senior writer, Lucien Rhodes, to write a full-blown article.

---

* New York: Doubleday Currency, 1992; paperback edition, 1994.

As is the case with many magazine articles, the piece that was eventually printed was a collective effort. Executive editor Bo Burlingham revised and rewrote Rhodes's draft and incorporated much of Amend's material about games. The article was printed in the magazine's August 1986 issue. Though it was titled "The Turnaround," it used the phrase "The Great Game of Business" to describe Stack's approach. ("Virtually everything that happens at SRC is based on the premise that business is essentially a game—one, moreover, that almost anyone can learn to play.") Later, Burlingham would collaborate with Stack on the 1992 book with that title.

Sports metaphors come easily to Stack. Business, he likes to say, is indeed just like any game. You have to know the rules and be able to follow the action. You have to have a chance to win or lose—meaning that you need a real stake in the outcome. "We all love to win," he'll say in one of his frequent speeches. "But we aren't interested in a game unless we understand it. How many people here know the rules of cricket? Do you think you'd really enjoy watching a cricket match—and don't forget, they can last for days—unless somebody taught you how the game was played?" If business is a game, the financials are the scorecard.

Anyway, when it came time to discuss SRC's elaborate system of meetings in their book, Stack and Burlingham christened the meetings *huddles*. The weekly company staff meeting was the "Great Huddle." Department meetings leading up to and following the Great Huddle were prehuddles and posthuddles.* Ironically, this nomenclature hasn't really caught on at SRC itself, where meetings are usually referred to as meetings. And plenty of companies have adopted the system without the names: Amoco Canada, for example, calls its open-book management meetings roundups, in keeping with the western flavor of its hometown (Calgary, Alberta). But many open-book companies do use the word *huddles*—and whatever you think of sports metaphors in general, it's a useful term because it means not just any old staff meeting.

> A huddle is a regular, structured series of meetings designed specifically to allow people to participate in running the business.

---

* For readers unacquainted with American football, the action in a football game occurs in a series of plays initiated by the offense—the team that has the ball. Before each play, offensive players gather in a circle, where they learn what the next play will be. That gathering is called a *huddle*.

Here's how the huddle system works at SRC. Each week, every business unit holds a meeting to review its performance for the past week. Departmental representatives arrive with key numbers in hand and report them at the meeting. Typically, the numbers are entered into a computer spreadsheet, and the spreadsheet is projected onto a screen so that everybody there can see it. In effect, a rudimentary income statement is created on the spot. But attendees are not merely examining last week's raw numbers; they're also reporting how they did compared to plan and discussing any variances that seem worth discussing. In addition, they're offering opinions as to what lies ahead—for the rest of the current month, at least, and often out into the next month or two. (Remember those forward-looking financials in Chapter 4!) The spreadsheet shows three numbers for every line item: *actual*, *plan*, and *opinion*.

At the end of the meeting, the financial report is printed out and distributed. Departmental reps—usually, but not always, the department manager—take them back for a posthuddle with everyone in the department. How are we doing in addressing these variances? What needs to be done to get ready for the rest of this month and for next month? Before the next huddle, a department may get together to report and examine its internal numbers (a prehuddle). People know that at the huddle they'll be expected to explain variances and have action plans at the ready. They know that they'll be accountable not only for their numbers, but for how the department (like any business) is preparing itself for the future.

The Huddle System at Work

Many companies have picked up on SRC's system, and, with variations, are utilizing it to run the business.

Mimi Taylor, manager of associate services, Vectra (Columbus, Ohio): "We have monthly companywide meetings and individual department meetings as often as each department deems it necessary. Some departments meet weekly, some meet biweekly, some even more frequently. At the monthly meeting, we're comparing plan to actual. We're talking about our performance and our operating income goal—where we are compared to our operating income goal, where we are to budget, and so on. We also have an opinion, like SRC. Opinion goes four weeks out: 'This is what our budget says we're going to do, but here's what the short term looks like.'

That's so we can make adjustments if that four weeks out doesn't look as good as the budget. Or if it looks better, what do we need to do to get ready for that?"

Bob Taylor, general manager, heavy-oil business unit, Amoco Canada (Calgary, Alberta): "We went and designed what we now call the roundup process. We have preroundup meetings and post-roundup meetings, and, of course, the roundup itself, which is the meeting with our senior executives. We told the executives we didn't want them just to take a sheet from their finance guy and bring it and say, "Well here's my guy's numbers," but that they were expected to come in, *present* those numbers, or at least bring their finance guy to present the numbers for them. They were expected to come in with a sense of ownership and understanding of where the numbers came from. Most of the units at that time adopted what we call a preroundup meeting, where the team leaders responsible for the income sets within the business unit—in our case that's six team leaders—have to present their share of the numbers. Then we add those up and have a tear sheet that we give to the vice president, and he can then take that forward as his share of the company's numbers. We're trying to create a more direct line of sight back down to the individual work teams."

Bill Friedman, co-owner, Cascade Bookkeeping (Bend, Oreg.): "We have a weekly staff meeting. It lasts an hour. We publish an agenda with a specific time frame for each item and a person assigned to that item. The two fixed items on the agenda are a financial review and projection. Our staff developed an operating plan for the year, and each person on staff is responsible for income items or expense items or both. We just go around the room; people report what they think the income for the month is going to be, what they think expenses are going to be, all compared to budget. Before the meeting, we distribute a work sheet, which shows where we are: a budget for each month and actuals for past months. We'll show what our prediction was last week. And then there's a blank column, which is, 'Here's what my prediction is for this week.' So we all get the opportunity to say what we think the numbers will be. Then, at the meeting, we come to a consensus and punch the numbers into the computer. Right after the meeting we distribute a copy of the printout to everybody. It's a simple spreadsheet."

Brent Youngblood, CFO, Crisp Publications (Menlo Park, Calif.):
"We close the books in five days. We give managers three days to re-view their ledger. If there are entries in there that don't make sense or that they think should be someone else's, then they let us know and we get it fixed. Then we have our huddle. It's a group of seven people getting together. Our culture has always been doing comparisons with last year, as opposed to SRC's approach, which is more forward thinking. Maybe we need to spend more time looking backward, because our business is different. We have tens of thousands of customers; the historical data tell us what to expect. But we also do a forecast at the meeting, and we compare actual against budget and actual against the last forecast. Then everybody gets a copy."

A manager at a large high-tech manufacturing company: "Our huddles take place monthly. Everyone within our business seg-ments—more than 700 people—is invited. We review the P&L for each product line, with projections for the current quarter, the next quarter, and the year. We have remote sites in three other places, spanning ten time zones, so at one place it's 4:30 in the afternoon and at another it's 6:30 in the morning. We use a teleconferencing setup for audio and MS Netmeeting software for the computer data. This allows us to run an Excel spreadsheet, which shows up on everybody's computer simultaneously. Initially, it took us most of a day to do all this, but now we have it down to two hours.
"The prehuddles within each product line are customized for each particular business. In the product line I'm associated with, the prehuddle is a three-hour meeting that goes through all the projects, the marketing and sales projections, and the financials, all in preparation for the main huddle. We're doing a much better job of staying on track to meet our financial goals since beginning regular huddles. We take steps to make corrections as soon as we see problems. When it looks like we're going to miss our goal, each product-line staff gets involved to seek out additional rev-enues from other sources, reduce or push out costs where possible, and use underutilized manufacturing capacity to build ahead. This latter action reduces our COGS significantly by improving our use of fixed costs. There are also the unmeasurable improvements that have come from getting people more involved. Employees constantly ask how we're doing toward meeting our financial goals and where we are relative to hitting the group-incentive payout-plan goal—and they usually have an idea that will help in some way."

Empowerment through Huddles

The goal of any huddle system is simple: to provide a systematic way by which people throughout a company can take joint responsibility—and hold each other accountable—for their business performance. But realizing that goal means more than just sitting down with a calendar and making up a schedule of meetings. Meetings, like numbers, are a double-edged sword. Sometimes they're the bane of a company's (and a businessperson's) existence. They drag on too long. They accomplish little. They serve primarily as a vehicle for posturing and politicking or for one-way communication from the boss to the peons. But meetings can also be a hugely efficient means of sharing information, developing ideas, and making group decisions. The trick with a huddle system is to maximize the benefits while minimizing the costs. Some tips from open-book companies:

Remember the discipline of meetings. It always astonishes me that otherwise savvy managers still call meetings with no agenda, no predefined objectives, and no time limit. Nobody in business should walk into a meeting without knowing what will be discussed and for how long. Nobody should walk into a meeting unprepared. The person in charge of the meeting has to encourage broad participation, stick to the time limits, and ask people to continue tangential discussions afterward, in private. Plenty of books and articles discuss how to make meetings productive; plenty of consultants can teach the necessary skills if they are needed. Properly conceived, meetings are not a distraction from work. They are a way of getting the work done.

The primary agenda of a huddle is to discuss the numbers. Regular staff meetings can and must take up a variety of concerns: longer-term matters such as hiring needs, near-term concerns such as vacation scheduling, and so on. But a huddle isn't a huddle unless it focuses on how we did last week (last month), what we think will happen this week (this month), and *what we have to do to make the numbers move in the right direction.* That's the central concern of any huddle. It means that the numbers have to be available, and that people need to know what they mean. It also means setting aside time for brainstorming about improving performance and dealing with what lies ahead—for the development of action plans.

People need to take ownership of the numbers. Before Amoco Canada started its roundup process, says Bob Taylor, "someone in accounting would give you your numbers—and then you'd spend the next week or so scrambling around trying to figure out why they were what they were." The situation may be similar at small companies. "Before, when you closed the books, you never saw the business unit managers," remembers Brent Youngblood, of Crisp Publications. "Now they're all over accounting. If a number's not right, they'll say, 'This number's not right! That's not my number!'"

Huddles have to take place regularly—and without fail. Skip a huddle or two and what happens? You miss the week's or month's updates, sure. But you also send a strong message to everyone in the organization: these meetings really aren't so important. Companies that have succeeded with huddles are companies that are religious about holding the meetings on schedule, with no skipping. That's what teaches people they're important.

As many people as possible should participate. Except in the smallest companies, it's impractical to assemble every employee in a company or business unit for more than occasional meetings. But everyone can take part in small-scale departmental or shift meetings, and everyone can take a turn attending higher-level meetings. Some companies open their huddles to anyone who wants to come. Others allow one representative in addition to the manager from each department and encourage departments to rotate their representation. That's how people learn what really happens. Huddles are a great teaching tool. As employees get up to speed at the meetings, they can be asked to report and explain their unit's numbers. It's another burden off the manager's back.

Supplement huddles with any other meetings you need to make things happen. Huddles are special-purpose meetings; they can't do the whole job alone. Sometimes units need to gather to discuss issues that can't be handled in the context of a regular weekly meeting. Sometimes they need to go off-site for a half-day or all-day retreat. A lot of companies ask their teams or departments to meet for a few minutes every day, just to map out the day's objectives and plans.

Communication with people who don't attend has to be fast and thorough. SRC and other companies print up the weekly or monthly financials, complete with comparisons and projections, literally on the spot. Huddle participants can take them back to their units for distribution and discussion. Communication has to go in the other direction, too. Departmental managers and reps should talk to folks in their unit. Is there anything that needs to be brought up at this week's huddle? What's our take on these numbers that I'm going to be reporting?

Huddles have to tie in with the rest of open-book management. The numbers that get the most scrutiny in a huddle are the company's— and the various departments'—critical numbers. The financials are often simplified, non-GAAP statements (which can be supplemented by a full close at month's end). New numbers can go up (or out) on the scoreboards after the huddles.

Huddles should generate some excitement. A huddle—where the numbers are revealed, projected, discussed—is where the people in a business see how they're faring. Those numbers *matter*. They're a cause for celebration, or for serious concern. Foldcraft Company puts on a whole show for its monthly meetings, holding them in a rented church hall. The executives dress up in black-and-white-striped referee uniforms, complete with whistles and yellow flags. ("We're attacking the bottom line at this meeting, not people," explains CFO Doug Westra. "If that starts happening, we call a foul.") Up on the wall, those four overhead projectors beam a horizontal income statement: actual numbers for the month and year to date, plan and current opinion as to upcoming months, all of it broken down by team. A display even shows the cost of the meeting— about $500, including refreshments and cash awards. The meeting lasts an hour. "One of our referees carries a stopwatch," says Westra. "We start at 2:30 and end at 3:30." In between? "It *moves*," he exclaims. "We have hooting and hollering and clapping. That's a big part of it—keeping the energy level high, just boom boom boom right down the line." After the first meeting, he adds, "I had so many people come up to me and say, 'Since I have been in the organization, that was the best thing we've ever done.'"

Foldcraft's style wouldn't work for every company. But a dull, dry review of the numbers isn't going to generate much excitement either. What's important isn't this or that gimmick, it's the feeling that a meeting generates. This is *our* company. These numbers are *our* numbers—and we're responsible for them. It's a whole different feeling from what you get from a suggestion system or some other partial form of empowerment.

Third Principle:
A Stake in Success

CHAPTER TEN

Overview: Bonuses, Good and Bad

I once sat next to a guy at a conference for *Inc.* 500 companies—companies that had qualified for *Inc.* magazine's annual list of the fastest-growing privately held businesses in the United States. We got to talking about bonuses, and he confided that his small manufacturing business had recently completed a pretty good year. So one afternoon he had passed out $10,000 checks to everybody on the shop floor.

Talk about a good day at work! This was a small, low-tech company in the rural South. For most employees, this wholly unexpected bonus must have amounted to half their annual wage. Other companies, too, sometimes pay generous bonuses, and not just on Wall Street (where a fat bonus is an expected part of the compensation package). Intel paid $820 million in profit sharing in 1996, an average of nearly $17,000 per employee, and in early 1997 announced that it would pay every worker a one-time thank-you bonus of $1,000.[*] Levi Strauss & Company announced in 1996 that if the company hit a cumulative cash-flow target of $7.6 billion in the next six years it would give every one of its 37,500 employees a full year's pay as a bonus. Benefits specialists, reported *Business Week*, said it may be "the richest and most unusual employee reward program ever."[†]

There's no doubt that bonus programs—and variable-compensation plans in general—are hot. Regular reports in the

---

[*] *Wall Street Journal*, February 12, 1997, p. B6.
[†] June 14, 1996, p. 44.

business press tell us that bonuses are no longer confined to the executive suites, that nearly half of U.S. companies either have a variable-comp plan in place or are considering instituting one, and that stock options are increasingly being used to reward all employees, not just top management. There are powerful forces behind this trend, so it seems likely to continue. Companies under severe competitive pressures—today this category includes most companies—are leery of giving out annual raises, which increase their fixed costs. They'd rather pay bonuses when times are good and nothing when times are hard. Companies also have begun to recognize the change in the nature of work discussed in Chapter 1. When jobs were simple and easily supervised, a manager didn't really care how the worker felt about the work. The only relevant message from management to employees was, Do your job, pick up your check, and if you don't do it right we'll find someone who will. Today, with supervisors scarce and jobs more complex, companies have to hope that employees *want* to do their jobs well. Variable-comp plans are supposed to provide an incentive for hard work and smart decisions.

Typically, however, these plans aren't worth the paper they're printed on, let alone the cost of the consultants who dream them up.

At most companies, nobody understands the bonus program. Employees don't know what bonuses are pegged to. (Profit goals? Revenue targets? How the boss is feeling the week before Christmas?) They don't know how the company is doing, so they have no idea whether there'll be a bonus at all. Nor do they understand how their own job contributes to (or hinders) corporate performance.

At one place where I used to work, for example, we'd get our bonus checks in early February—*if* we got them. Nobody knew ahead of time whether there would be a bonus, or how much it would be. Some years the bonus was pretty generous—about 10 percent of salary at my level, more than that for my bosses. Other years the bonus was zero. Management would explain to us that it had been a good year or a bad year or an okay year, which was supposed to explain why the bonus was what it was. Like employees everywhere, some of us took it on faith that management was telling the truth. The others scoffed at the whole thing. (They'll pay us whatever they want to pay us.) (This is not so far from the situation Levi Strauss employees are in. Though the company set a cash-flow goal as the trigger for paying the bonus, it declined to reveal what its *current* cash flow was. And who beyond a few senior managers knows how to affect cash flow anyway?)

In such a situation, the very best a bonus program can do is make you feel good about the company you work for. When somebody hands you a check for a few thousand extra dollars, you're inclined to feel, gee, this is a pretty good place to work after all. On the other hand, those warm fuzzies can evaporate as quickly as they appear. If there's no check for a few thousand dollars—of if the check is for a few hundred dollars when you expected a few thousand—it's hard to avoid the feeling that, gee, you've been screwed once again. If you get a few thousand dollars (good) and you hear that your manager got ten times that much (not so good—he's a jerk), you're likely to decide that the bonus program (like everything else in the world) is a stacked deck. Meanwhile, the other possible benefits of a bonus program, such as encouraging people to work smarter, are lost. How can people work to boost profits if they don't know what profits are or how any given job helps improve them?

Open-book companies take a different approach to variable compensation. Their bonus plans aren't just grafted on to the organization by some compensation consultant, they're an integral part of the whole management system. The bonus plan is expected not only to motivate employees but to help them learn. It's also expected to leave the company stronger at the end of the year than it was at the start, specifically because of the bonus. Let's examine each of these objectives in turn.

A piece of the action. An open-book bonus plan isn't an afterthought. It isn't charity. And it isn't even close to being "extra" that gets distributed because the owners or senior executives happen to be feeling generous. The bonus in open-book companies is an agreed-upon part—a significant part—of everyone's compensation package. It pays out only if the company or business unit hits certain goals, which are determined and spelled out in advance. The bonus is everybody's reward for boosting the company's performance—for succeeding in business. It's what makes it possible for employees in open-book companies to think of themselves as businesspeople. If you get paid the same whether your business does well or poorly, you aren't really in business. You're a hired hand.

Right away you can see a couple of conditions that an open-book bonus plan must meet. For one thing, it has to be generous—generous enough to matter. If the company is doing well, the bonus has to be a noticeable fraction of an employee's annual income. It also has to be both inclusive and fair. A bonus plan that leaves out any group of regular employees runs counter to the basic ideas of open-book management. So does a plan with widely disparate rewards. ("Nobody wants to come to work every day just to make the boss rich," says Jim Siegel of Hexacomb Corp.) And if you're figuring on using a bonus as a substitute for base pay, forget it; there's no faster way to turn employees into cynics than to hold back part of their pay. A bonus is an addition to competitive base pay. If business conditions require pay cuts, call them what they are: pay cuts.

The bonus as an educational tool. Open-book companies need their employees to understand some business basics, such as how the company makes money and what the critical numbers are that they can affect. Nobody learns as fast as a person who has real money at stake. "If you tell people that the payout is based partly on the current ratio," says Paul Centenari, president of Atlas Container Corporation in Odenton, Maryland, "then they'll become like certified public accountants—they'll know *everything* that goes into a current ratio."

Take Physician Sales & Service, the medical-supply distributing company, which has branches throughout the United States. PSS pays out bonuses to employees based on their branch's financial performance. The company measures that performance by several different indicators. One of these indicators is asset days.

On the surface, this measure is something only an accountant could love. To calculate it, you first have to figure your average daily sales. Then you divide that number into your accounts receivable balance at the end of the month, getting your accounts-receivable days. Next, you figure your average daily cost of sales and divide that into your average inventory balance, yielding inventory days. Finally, you add up accounts-receivable days and inventory days and—presto—you get asset days.

What this seemingly arcane number tells you, though, is how well you're managing your inventory and receivables. So it's a critically important metric for any distribution business with a lot of items on the shelves and a long list of customers.

Granted, probably not everybody in a PSS warehouse would know the whole formula for calculating asset days. But the fact that the bonus payout depends on a target for asset days communicates in no uncertain terms that this is a very important number—and people do understand that moving that number in the right direction depends on keeping inventory lean and receivables up-to-date. So what's the effect? Suddenly truck drivers and salespeople (who deal with customers) care about the same thing receivables clerks care about, namely, getting those accounts paid up. Suddenly warehouse workers have to concern themselves with inventory accuracy. They learn what's important to PSS's business.

If a bonus is going to be an educational tool, of course, it has to be coupled with instruction, reminders, and communication. That's another reason for teaching the business, setting up scoreboards, and doing everything else involved with open-book management. Some companies—Bonanza Nut & Bolt, for example—even track employees' progress toward the bonus on the scoreboard (Chapter 5).

Making the company stronger. Most companies have weaknesses or vulnerabilities in any given year. They have poor inventory accuracy. They can't seem to get their on-time delivery up to par. They're too reliant on one product line. They're facing a cash crunch, budget cuts, or a new competitive challenge. These are the problems that keep managers awake at night—and that they rarely share with employees. But what happens if you identify a weakness, set a goal for improvement, and then peg at least part of the bonus payout to hitting that goal? Bingo: now everybody in the company is worrying about that problem and working to rectify it. And if people can't affect the problem directly, they're at least helping out and cheering on the people who can.

"A good bonus program," wrote Jack Stack in an influential article in *Inc.* magazine, "is a kind of insurance policy. It gets everyone involved in going after a company's greatest weakness." Usually, added Stack, a weakness can be expressed in the form of a financial ratio—but "you don't start with the ratio." Instead, you ask people to talk about what they see as the company's biggest threats and vulnerabilities, then home in on what managers and employees agree is the most critical one. "In effect, you put a bounty on that number and say, 'By hitting these targets we can drive out this big weakness out and strengthen the company, and so we're going to give ourselves a reward if we do it.'"*

---

* "The Problem with Profit-Sharing," *Inc.*, November 1996, pp. 67–69.

Company owners and managers naturally worry about bonuses. What if we can't afford to pay one—won't the whole program be demotivating? What if people come to believe that they're entitled to a bonus—doesn't it stop being an effective incentive? In conventional companies these are real concerns. People don't know whether or why they're being paid a bonus and naturally feel they're being shafted if they don't get one. But a well-crafted open-book bonus plan, unlike conventional plans, doesn't run into these problems. People can see how the company is doing on the bonus measures as the year unfolds. If the company can't afford the bonus, that fact will come as no surprise. As employees come to see themselves as businesspeople, they'll have a businesslike attitude toward the variable part of their compensation. They *will* feel entitled to a bonus, rightly, if their business is successful. They won't if it isn't.

Nevertheless, there are plenty of issues to be considered in open-book bonus design, and the rest of this section gets into the nuts and bolts. Chapters 11 and 12 lay out the issues, including the issue of how to encourage long-term concern for the business, which is inextricably tied up with employee stock ownership. Chapter 13, a collection of mini-examples, shows how ten different companies solved ten different problems arising from bonus-plan design. If they fit your company, steal the ideas. They work.

Bonus Design: Part One

What you want an open-book bonus system to do is pretty simple: focus everyone's attention on the critical elements of business performance and thereby build a stronger, more profitable company. Stronger companies provide more job security and more opportunities. They generate more wealth to share. So everybody in the company has a powerful interest in establishing a bonus program that *works*—that does what it's supposed to do. A program that works helps people understand those critical goals. It helps them learn how they can move the numbers in the right direction. It should lead to better performance. In effect, it changes a company's whole organizational logic.

Organizational logic? Sure. Take Commercial Casework, for example. Located in Fremont, California, Commercial Casework manufactures architectural casework. It's a job shop: all its products are custom-built. Business is good for the company when

- it has plenty of *sales*—completed jobs are humming out the door and revenue is flowing in;

- it has a healthy *backlog*—when any job is complete, there are plenty of others waiting to be built;

- it has a good, solid *average gross margin*—its salespeople haven't bid too low; its designers and purchasers have kept materials costs under control; its production people and installation teams get jobs done on time and on, or under, budget. Remember president Bill Palmer's dictum (Chapter 3): "We're in a labor-intensive tight-margin industry. . . . A little improvement in gross margin . . . makes a huge difference to the bottom line."

If Commercial Casework weren't an open-book company, who would be concerned with these three numbers? The owners, sure. Senior managers, probably—at least you would hope so. But not many others. Salespeople, like salespeople everywhere, would be watching their own top line. Engineers and designers would concern themselves with the elegance of their designs—and would be in perennial conflict with the folks in purchasing, who would be carping about materials costs. Production and installation crews wouldn't know the budget for each job; they'd just be putting in their hours and doing what they were told. (Production *supervisors* might be concerned with making budget, but probably not with beating it.) Everyone downstream from sales would be hoping that business wasn't *too* good, so there wouldn't be more work to be done in a day—except that some hourly people would be hoping for enough work to generate overtime pay (and if that dented the gross margin on a job, so what?). Conventional companies are collections of individual fiefdoms. Everyone watches out for his or her own interests.

But when Commercial Casework went open-book, it set up a bonus plan around those three critical numbers: sales, backlog, and average gross margin. Each number had a target for the year. If the company hit all three targets, everybody would get a bonus. Did employees suddenly begin thinking and acting differently? Not right away; people are people, and change their behavior only slowly. What did happen, though, was that the organizational logic of Commercial Casework began to shift. People now had a sense that there were new objectives, objectives that they had in common with others in the company. They began to learn what their role was in reaching the objectives. In discussions about pricing, salespeople couldn't lobby too hard for lowball bidding, because it would screw up gross margin. Design and purchasing people realized they had to work together to keep costs low. Production and installation crews began to look at the budgets for jobs—and to challenge themselves to beat the budgets, thereby increasing margin.

In effect, Commercial Casework was giving individuals a chance to shine by helping the company reach its objectives. Salespeople who brought in big new jobs were heroes; those jobs helped the company hit its monthly revenue and backlog targets. Anybody who contributed to a better gross margin—figuring out a way to reduce direct costs, getting a job done faster than expected—was a hero, too. In most companies, the organizational logic is, You do your job and I'll do mine and let's hope we don't get in each other's hair too much. In an open-book company, such as Commercial Casework, the organizational logic is, We're in this together because we have the same goals. The bonus reinforces that new organizational logic.

To be sure, it's one thing to change the way a company is supposed to work. It's another thing entirely to change the way people actually think and act. That takes time—and it takes careful attention to the details of matters such as a bonus program.

The Employee-Designed Bonus

The first step in designing an open-book bonus program is to assemble a committee of volunteers—people who are willing to take on the job of figuring out the bonus.

Now, this may seem like a pretty radical step. Traditionally, bonus plans are designed by compensation consultants or senior management and are then announced to the troops. That works fine if you don't expect the troops to understand or care about the bonus; it doesn't work so well if you do. Get people involved from the beginning and three good things happen: (1) the participants learn a helluva lot; (2) you get input and feedback from the people who will be affected; (3) the involvement of line employees makes a better and more credible plan. If you're a member of a bonus committee, you'll have to figure out what your company's critical numbers are, how much of a bonus the company can reasonably afford, and what kind of a payout system seems fair. You'll have to understand the options so you can explain them to your associates. You'll also want the plan to be something you *can* defend. That means you'll want it to be fair, generous, and easily comprehensible—essential characteristics of an open-book plan.

It's a good idea for senior managers to be involved as well, of course. Senior managers are likely to know more about the finances of the company, and hence about what's possible. Then, too, a company isn't a democracy; it's the owners' money that's at risk, and whatever the employee committee comes up with will have to be okayed by whoever is in charge. That's easier if the folks in charge are in on the discussion from the start.

Larger organizations may need a compensation consultant as well. But the consultant's role is not to design a plan, even less to install a prepackaged one. It's to explain alternatives, help people focus on key issues, make sure whatever plan people come up with meshes with the company's existing compensation system and doesn't run afoul of the law.

(Speaking of the law, note that U.S. labor law hasn't yet caught up with open-book management; it's actually illegal for management to establish a joint employer-employee committee that negotiates a binding agreement regarding compensation. It is not illegal, however, to ask representative employees to sit on a compensation advisory committee. If your company is likely to show up on the National Labor Relations Board's radar screen, check with a labor lawyer to be sure you're staying within the law.)

Companies establish their committees in a variety of ways. Arning Industries, in Cassville, Missouri, set up a committee with two representatives elected from the ranks of hourly employees and two from salaried employees. At Commercial Casework, CEO Palmer assembled a group of six volunteers from different departments and met with them one afternoon a week for eight weeks. Between meetings, they were charged with gathering input from other employees. In the discussions, Palmer himself urged the importance of pegging a bonus to gross margin, explaining how important that number was to the company's pretax profit, and to sales volume. Another member of the group pointed out the importance of backlog. When the details of the plan were decided, Palmer introduced it at a monthly meeting and passed out a memo explaining it. Group members met with other employees in small groups to answer questions.

You'd expect employees to come up with more generous bonus plans than would owners or managers. For reasons I don't entirely understand, the opposite is more common. "The bonus plan our employee committee came up with was much tougher than the one our CFO and I came up with," says Richard Weiss, president of Mountain Travel Sobek, an adventure-travel company in El Cerrito, California. "The threshold [for payout] was higher. It was more generous to the owners than we had originally planned."

Setting Goals

What should trigger a bonus payout?

This is really two questions. The first has to do with what variables the bonus should be pegged to. Net profit? Return on assets? Something else entirely? The second question is how high the targets should be set. We'll take these up in turn.

Net profit versus performance drivers

Most so-called bonus plans, as Stack pointed out in his *Inc.* article, are really just profit-sharing plans. If the company makes enough money, a portion of the earnings is distributed to the employees. So *profit* is what triggers the payout.

A profit-sharing plan is a nice benefit, but by itself it has little effect on how people work. It doesn't teach people *why* profits are up or down. It doesn't help them understand what has to happen or what they can do to improve profit performance. An open-book bonus plan *can* be pegged to net profit—many are—but only if the relationship between what people do on the job and how much money the company makes is easily understood.

That's the case in some small companies. Take Smith & Company Engineers, for example, in Poplar Bluff, Missouri. The company has only 35 employees, all of them engineers or support staff. It makes money when, and only when, those engineers are working on billable projects. The scoreboard is posted every day; it lists every individual's total hours, billable hours, and dollars billed, all compared to a monthly target. The more billable hours, the higher Smith & Company's profits. The company's bonus plan can be pegged to profits because all the employees know exactly how they can contribute to the bottom line.

In larger organizations, it's almost always more effective to target not profit per se but *performance drivers*. This is not just a matter of semantics. Profit, after all, is only one goal among many for a business. In any given year it may not be the top priority. Sales growth, new-product development, or half a dozen other objectives may be more important. Figuring out your performance drivers forces you to ask, What is our most important measure of performance *this year*?

When RR Donnelley & Sons' Northeastern Division set up teams to work on a bonus plan, one team was charged with precisely this question (Chapter 20). Explains Don Robb, who coordinates the open-book effort for the division: "Their role was to respond to the statement, 'A successful 1997 depends on improving our performance in these key areas of our business.' Which areas? And what are the variables that drive performance in those areas?"

Another approach to figuring out performance drivers: examine your company's weaknesses and vulnerabilities. Share Group, a telephone marketing and fund-raising company, recognized that it had a high cost structure (because it paid relatively high wages and benefits) and was in danger of being undercut in the marketplace by competitors. The solution: a bonus plan pegged to keeping labor costs low as a percentage of sales.

If you read Chapter 3 (and I hope you did) you will recognize that performance drivers are your company's critical numbers for the year. To repeat two sentences: Critical numbers are the numbers that drive a business's key objectives. They're the numbers that must move in the right direction if the business is to succeed in what it is trying to do *right now*. Critical numbers, performance drivers—whatever you call them, these should be the primary focus of a bonus plan. An effective plan rewards people for moving these numbers in the right direction.

Gates and multiple objectives

Bonuses don't have to be pegged to one goal. You're probably better off targeting at least two goals, sometimes more. There are three reasons.

One reason is that you're likely to need a *gate*—a go–no go switch that determines whether any bonus at all will be paid out. The purpose of a gate is to make sure the company really can afford a bonus. It acknowledges the sad reality that a business can improve its performance in all the key areas and still find itself in trouble for reasons beyond its control. Maybe prices have plummeted. Maybe the market has shifted in some other way.

Profit level is an obvious gate. Electronic Controls Company (ECCO), in Boise, Idaho, puts nothing into its bonus pool until profit exceeds 4 percent. The employees of Amoco Canada, in Calgary, were to get no bonus in 1996 unless both Amoco Canada and parent Amoco Corporation hit threshold targets for return on capital employed. In small companies, cash levels, or some measure of cash availability, such as the current ratio, may be a necessary gate. You shouldn't be in the position of owing a bonus that you don't have the cash to pay for.

A second reason for a gate: no business is one-dimensional. Usually you have to improve performance on a couple or three different dimensions if you really want to strengthen your company. Commercial Casework needed three goals. RR Donnelley focused on two drivers for each of the Northeastern Division's four business modules. Jim's Formal Wear pays a portion of profits into its bonus pool, but the exact percentage received by each facility depends on that facility's performance on measures of labor efficiency and quality. Multiple objectives encourage people to learn more about the business.

A final reason: establishing multiple objectives is the only way around two common bonus-plan pitfalls. I think of them as the *sphere-of-control* issue and the *local versus corporate* issue.

Plenty of companies (though not many open-book ones) pay a bonus according to some purely operational measure of performance, such as units shipped, or quality. Proponents of this kind of metric argue that employees have no real control over financial performance. The bottom line depends on too many variables, many of them external to the shop floor. What is within their sphere of control is what happens *on* the shop (or office) floor. So they should be rewarded for their performance in getting goods out the door.

This is the thinking behind conventional gain-sharing plans, and it sounds appealing. Why penalize people who are working hard because something beyond their control undermined their performance? Trouble is, that's exactly what happens in business. You bust your butt, you do everything you're supposed to do, and surprise! you find you're not making any money because a competitor recently came out with a better product. If employees are to be businesspeople, they have to learn that lesson, which means that no company should be paying a bonus when its financial performance is poor. By all means, target operational measures if they are your business's critical numbers. But link those targets to financial ones so that you don't find yourself in a position of paying a bonus that you can't afford—or, worse, *not* paying a bonus that employees believe they have earned.

Much the same thinking applies to the issue of local versus companywide goals. In a large corporation, the bottom line is well beyond most employees' line of sight. (It may be hard enough to see how your own job relates to the performance of your own business unit, but establishing that connection is at least manageable.) So paying a bonus based on corporate performance alone attenuates any connection between accomplishments and rewards. On the other hand, no company wants to pay fat bonuses to people in one division when the rest of the corporation is struggling. So the two measures have to be combined into one. Crisp Publications, for example, pays half its bonus on business-unit earnings, half on consolidated corporate earnings. The bonus received by employees of Donnelley's Northeastern Division depends half on companywide performance and half on their own business unit's performance.

How high the targets?

How high is reasonable? Targets that are easily reachable won't do much to improve the company's performance. Targets that are too high—that seem impossible—will make the whole bonus plan seem like a sham. A rule of thumb: the targets that trigger a bonus payout should be a stretch, but should be eminently reachable. Better to err on the low side than on the high, in my view—you can always increase the targets next year.

Of course, targets are typically set by negotiation and compromise—all the more reason to have employee representatives involved in designing the bonus. A business unit of one large company set its targets between historical performance (perceived as easily able to be duplicated) and budgeted performance goals as set by the corporate office (perceived as wholly impossible by the local folks). At Commercial Casework, the company achieved all its goals during the first year of the bonus plan, and when a new employee committee convened to discuss the next year's plan, they figured they'd just leave the goals where they were. CEO Bill Palmer refused to go along—this was about performance improvement, not performance maintenance—and showed the committee that the company had been performing at a substantially higher level during the last six months of the year than during the first. People figured that they could certainly equal that level during the coming year and agreed to set the targets accordingly.

A rule of thumb: if no one can convincingly explain *how* the company can reach the goals that trigger a payout, the goals are too high.

Creating the Bonus Pool

Let's say your company hits its targets. How much money will be distributed as bonuses? There are two ways of figuring it. You can pay everyone a fixed amount—usually a predetermined percentage of a person's total wages or salary—if the company makes bonus and nothing if it doesn't. This in some ways is the simplest approach: you set goals, then develop a budget that includes a bonus if the goals are met. If the company reaches its goals, you know you have the money to pay out the bonuses because it's all in the budget. What should the percentage be? That depends on your company's financial situation, the marketplace in which you compete, and several other variables. It should be as generous as you can afford. Crisp Publications pays 15 percent of salary across the board. Other companies have two, three, or more gradations.

We'll discuss the pros and cons of more-equal versus less-equal payouts in the next chapter. For the moment, consider the pros and cons of the fixed-payout, all-or-nothing approach. Employees have a big incentive to do everything they can to make sure the company makes bonus—and not much incentive to do more. That puts a premium on astute planning and goal setting and suits companies that can forecast their year's performance with a high degree of accuracy. It doesn't suit companies whose fortunes may swing substantially one way or the other in the course of a year. (I'm thinking of small businesses dependent on a few large customers, companies with new and untested products or services, companies in highly volatile markets, and so forth.) If they don't come close to their goals, the bonus plan seems fraudulent. If they greatly exceed their goals, people feel that they're "only" getting a fixed bonus and aren't really sharing in the company's success.

The alternative, of course, is to create a bonus pool, whose size depends on the company's performance. Bonuses can range from zero to anything at all (though many companies impose a cap).

How to structure such a pool? Most companies that take this approach devise some kind of formula.

- RR Donnelley's Northeastern Division creates a pool from savings on two operational measures, then pays out a certain percentage of the pool every quarter. The payout percentage is determined by a business unit's overall financial performance for the quarter. (See Chapter 13.)

- Bagel Works, a chain of stores headquartered in Keene, New Hampshire, puts 23 percent of net earnings over budget into a bonus pool every four weeks.

- Hexacomb Corporation, a manufacturer with seven plants in the United States, splits over-budget profits 50–50 with employees, but employees collect a bonus only if *their* plant beats its budget (Chapter 13.)

- Heflin Steel Company, in Phoenix, sets a series of profit targets for its companywide gain-sharing program and gives employees an extra day's wages for each level the company hits. In each of the last two years, the company paid out more than 50 extra days' pay—a bonus of over 20 percent.

The pool approach has several advantages. It's not an all-or-nothing system. It can accommodate fluctuation in the business's fortunes. If the company does exceptionally well, everybody does exceptionally well. The more money a company makes, of course, the more generous it can afford to be with bonuses. Thus S&R Industries, in Baker City, Oregon, puts from 20 to 50 percent of its profits into a bonus pool. Several other open-book companies follow this kind of formula as well.

The bucket plan

You won't find a simpler variable-pool system than the bucket plan devised by Steve Wilson of Mid-States Technical and subsequently adopted by several open-book companies. I described Wilson's plan in *Open-Book Management: The Coming Business Revolution.* I later learned that Smith & Company Engineers had created one much like it.

Conventional bonus plans pay out at the end of a fixed time period—every quarter, say, or every year. A bucket plan, in contrast, pays off whenever a company "fills a bucket" by earning a predetermined amount of profits. In Smith & Company's plan, dubbed "A Bigger Bucket of Bucks," the year's first $50,000 in profits was the first bucket. The second and third buckets were also $50,000, but every bucket after that was only $25,000. So if the company earned $200,000 in profits, it would have filled five buckets.

Each bucket contributed an agreed-upon percentage to a bonus pool. Smith & Company's first bucket paid 25 percent, or $12,500, into the pool. The second and third buckets paid 30 percent, or $15,000, into the pool. With later buckets, the percentage rose sharply, to as high as 85 percent. So there was a strong incentive to keep filling buckets.

The people at Mid-States Technical got pretty excited about their plan; at one point employees were laying odds on when the next bucket would be filled. Owner Samuel Smith of Smith & Company is happy with his plan, too. "This is our third year," he said in 1996. "Everybody's into it here! The conversation is, 'When are we going to make a bucket?'"

Bonus Design: Part Two

Whenever you establish a bonus plan, you uncover any number of issues. Who's included? How should the pool be divided up? When should the bonus be paid out? These (and many other) questions don't always have easy or obvious answers. This chapter takes up several of the issues you'll have to resolve in order to create a successful bonus plan, and describes how open-book companies have addressed them.

Who's Included?

The simplest answer to this question is "everyone." But the world is never so simple. What about temps? Part-timers? New employees? People who leave before the year is complete? Most companies require a probationary period—anywhere from three months to a year—before an employee can be included in the bonus plan, and most don't pay bonuses to people who leave during the year. You'll have to make a series of administrative decisions that suit your situation. (Commercial Casework had to figure out what to do about an employee who left and then returned in the same year.) One company's bonus memo is more or less typical: "All [company] office employees who work at least 20 hours a week in the office and have been employed in the [company] office for three continuous months or more will be eligible for the bonus plan. All office staff will be treated equally under the plan." (Don't be thrown off by the phrase "office employees." It's not to distinguish office from factory employees; office employees are the only kind of employees this company has. But the company engages a lot of contract personnel, who are not covered by the bonus.)

Beyond administrative choices, two issues arise. What about senior executives? And what about salespeople?

Senior executives—CEOs in particular—are sometimes left out of the company bonus plan and rewarded (usually more generously) according to a plan of their own. I think this is a mistake. The whole purpose of an open-book bonus plan is to get everyone in the business focused on the same objectives. To reward the CEO for an increase in, say, stock value and everybody else for an increase in, say, gross margin communicates exactly the wrong message, which is that the boss will worry about getting the ball in the cup while the rest of you folks should just keep your heads down and your arms straight. People with different jobs and people in different departments may be responsible for different targets and may have *part* of their bonus pegged to objectives for which they are uniquely responsible. But everybody, CEO included, should be rewarded for attaining some common objectives. They should all be in the same plan.

Salespeople are sometimes left out of companywide bonus plans as well. Salespeople work on commission, the theory runs. They generally get bonuses (and spiffs and prizes and awards and trips) of their own. This is another mistake. How many companies have found themselves in trouble precisely because salespeople are reading from one page of music and everybody else is reading from another? When salespeople concern themselves only with top-line revenues, bad things happen. They give discounts too freely. They become too turf conscious. They promise more than the company can deliver (and then try to cajole the production folks into making *their* customers a priority). Some open-book companies—ECCO, for example—have gone so far as to put all salespeople on salary, abolishing commissions entirely. Others have changed from commissions based on revenues to commissions based on gross margin. Whatever they do about sales compensation overall, though, most make sure to include salespeople in the bonus system. It's the only way to get everybody playing the same tune.

Some open-book companies add a nice little twist to the who's included question: they ask eligible employees to learn a little more about open-book management in order to receive their bonus. Commercial Casework pays a bonus to employees who "work a minimum of 400 hours per quarter and complete the continuing education requirements." In 1997, those requirements included reading a book on open-book management and attending in-house courses on the company's finances and business. Bagel Works sends out a quiz based on the current financials at the end of each bonus period; pass the quiz and you get your bonus. (Sample questions: "How do you arrive at cost of goods?" "What is our ideal payroll percent number?") It's an open-book test. (Naturally.)

Figuring Relative Shares

If you have a fixed-payout, all-or-nothing plan—so much percent of salary—you have to decide whether to pay everyone the same percentage or to pay different percentages to people with different jobs. If you have a pool plan—everyone gets a share of a varying total—you have to decide the rules for divvying it up. The problem is the same in both cases. Should people get more- or less-equal shares? What factors should be taken into account in making the distribution? Open-book companies take four different approaches.

Equal shares. A few open-book companies divide the bonus pool exactly equally, which means, of course, that lower-paid employees get a higher percentage of their salaries in bonus than do higher-paid employees. Many more use this equality principle as one factor in a hybrid scheme.

Proportional shares. This approach is the most common: everybody gets the same percentage of gross W-2 earnings in bonus. The calculation is as simple with a pool approach as it is with a fixed-payout plan: you total up the pool, calculate what percentage of eligible payroll the pool represents, then pay that amount.

Stepwise division. Same idea as proportional shares—people get a percentage of their W-2 earnings—but the percentages vary depending on jobs and responsibilities. SRC has its two categories, with maximum payouts of 13 and 18 percent. Another open-book company has a series of steps, from 10 percent, for hourly workers, to 50 percent, for top executives. Commercial Casework pays 100 shares of the bonus pool to each regular employee. Apprentices get 60 or 80 shares depending on their experience. Team leaders get 120, supervisors 140, and managers 160.

    This is a tough nut! Proponents of higher rewards for managers argue that people who take on extra responsibilities deserve extra rewards. Those who pay proportional shares argue that managers already get higher pay and so get higher bonuses; they don't need to be paid a higher *percentage* of salary in bonus. They also point out how easily a stepwise system can backfire. One software company, for instance, launched a system in which line employees were eligible for one share from the pool, team leaders for two shares, and the management team three shares. "They weren't happy with that!" recalled one chagrined manager, referring to the people at the bottom of the scale. (Indeed, the system provoked so many comments that the company promptly changed it.)

You'll have to decide what's right for your company on this score. What's *wrong* for your company is a bonus system that's felt to be somehow unfair. This is not a matter of numbers, it's a matter of attitudes. Few line employees begrudge their bosses a higher salary *if* they feel that the bosses are worthy of respect *and* that they earn that salary. They may buy the idea of higher (relative) bonuses, too, if there's a good business rationale for it. What people won't buy is disparities that seem arbitrary or out of proportion to differing levels of responsibility.

Hybrid systems. Many open-book companies devise rules of their own for divvying up the bonus—rules that incorporate any number of criteria. ECCO takes the bonus pool and divides it into three parts. The first is allocated equally, the second by salary, and the third by length of service. The system, explains president Ed Zimmer, builds in the fundamental value of equal sharing, but also rewards contribution (measured by salary) and longevity with the company. Mid-States Technical divides 35 percent of its buckets equally and 65 percent according to salary. "We feel that everyone makes some equal contribution to the company," says founder Steve Wilson; this way, he adds, lower-paid employees wind up with a higher percentage of their pay in the form of a bonus.

Another form of hybrid combines individual-performance ratings with a companywide bonus plan. Vectra won't pay a bonus to employees on probation. Physician Sales & Service salespeople don't get a bonus unless they have hit their individual sales targets. Bay State Press, in Framingham, Massachusetts, has a system in which every employee signs an individual-performance contract listing objectives to be accomplished in a given quarter; individual bonuses depend partly on how many objectives an employee accomplishes.

Whatever you decide, it's wise to run the distribution plan by a labor or benefits attorney. Labor law again: if you have hourly employees, you may have to add the bonus to the base wage, figure out the "new" hourly rate including the bonus, then recalculate and pay a new overtime rate for every individual.

Timing the Payout

Traditional bonuses were paid annually, usually around Christmastime, or maybe in February, after the year's books were closed. A few open-book companies continue this practice and pay bonuses in fat, once-a-year chunks. This is most common when a business is highly seasonal, as with agricultural-supply companies and retailers that do half their annual business in the months between Labor Day and Christmas. If your sales swing drastically from one quarter to the next, it makes little sense to pay bonuses based on an individual quarter's performance. It may even undermine the power of the bonus. "Last year we handed the bonuses out by quarter," reports vice president Dan Schweitzer of Docu-Net Inc., in Brookfield, Wisconsin. "We got well ahead, handed out a lot, then had a slow period in the summer. The rest of the year there was no chance to get anything. It's kind of a downer—plus it eats into your cash flow. So this year we decided to do it only at the end of the year."

Most open-book companies, however, do pay bonuses more frequently: quarterly, bimonthly, or even monthly. The thinking is simple: it's hard to get too excited about playing a game that pays off only once a year. More-frequent payments keep the bonus—and the performance measures on which the bonus is based—closer to the forefront of everyone's mind.

Wisconsin Label Company, in Algoma, Wisconsin, takes the more-frequent-is-better approach to its logical conclusion and pays a bonus every month. Company president Terry Fulwiler holds a monthly STP (share the profit) meeting in the 600-employee company's warehouse. He puts the income statement (actuals and plan) on an overhead projector, leads discussions on particularly good or bad line items, reveals the bottom line for the month, and passes out bonus checks on the spot. "All month, people are aware of what kind of track we're on," he says. "Near the end, everybody gets excited wondering what the bonus will be." What if Wisconsin Label has a losing month? Not only is there no bonus, says

Fulwiler, but the loss has to be made up before any bonus can be paid next month.

A more typical approach is to pay quarterly and to hold back some of the bonus that is earned each quarter as a kind of insurance policy against bad quarters in the remainder of the year. Woodpro Cabinetry, in Cabool, Missouri, pays out 65 percent of any bonus earned during a quarter and holds back 35 percent until the end of the following quarter. SRC developed the 10–20–30–40 formula followed by a lot of open-book companies. The company's budget shows what the total bonus will be if it hits its goals for the year. If it hits the first-quarter goals, it pays out 10 percent of the total. If it hits the second-quarter goals, it pays out 20 percent of the total, and so on, with 30 percent in the third quarter and 40 percent in the fourth. The system is cumulative; if SRC misses its goals in the first quarter, there'll be no bonus, but if it recovers, and hits year-to-date goals at the end of the second quarter, employees get the full 30 percent for the first two quarters. The effect, says Jack Stack, is to keep people in the game all year. Even if things have been going badly, they can pull out a full bonus if they can somehow turn it around later in the year.

How soon after the close of a quarter (or month, or year) should the bonus be paid? Share Group, in Somerville, Massachusetts, at one point got itself into trouble because it was paying periodic bonuses based on profits well before it had collected the cash from sales for that period of time. Result: a cash-flow crunch. Now Share pays its bonuses 45 days after the close of a bonus period—about the time it takes for the company to collect. If you peg bonus payouts to average receivable days, you help ensure the availability of cash—and you give everyone a quick lesson in that all-important difference between profit and cash.

Celebrations

It shouldn't need saying, but it does: when you pay a bonus, put on a party! "Set up booths for check distribution and combine it with a celebration," writes compensation expert Jerry L. McAdams, "anything from coffee and doughnuts to a picnic. I know a CEO who has a stack of checks . . . and hands them out, with her thanks, to each of the people at the event."*

---

* *The Reward Plan Advantage* (San Francisco: Jossey-Bass Publishers, 1996), p. 298.

Conventional companies rarely follow this precept. Typically, they give people an extra check or deposit memo with their regular paycheck or simply figure the bonus in and give people a single, bigger check. Open-book companies are more likely to celebrate, often with flair. Controller Fred Saul of Bay State Press dressed up like the money man in Monopoly when he passed out the company's first bonus checks. Docu-Net Inc. pays its bonuses annually, but passes out $100 quarter prizes if employees hit a target, such as a certain percent billable hours, and in 1996 made a point of passing out the newly redesigned $100 bills. Carolyn Chandler, owner of Chandler Properties in San Francisco, "popped four bottles of champagne" at the first bonus meeting. A Chicago company—requesting anonymity for fear of getting in trouble with the National Basketball Association—staged a presentation, complete with music and lights, modeled on the introduction of the Chicago Bulls before a basketball game. Other companies put on picnics, produce skits, or just throw a party.

The fact is, of course, you don't have to be paying out bonus checks to have fun. Rhino Foods, in Burlington, Vermont, holds Rhino Day once a year. The company shuts down for a day, and everybody gets together for contests, slide shows, music, and food. Still, if there's some money to be passed out, it adds to the occasion.

Reassessment—and Change

McAdams also emphasizes regular reassessment of the bonus system. "For heaven's sake, re-evaluate!" he exclaims. "Constantly assess how well you're doing. If the bonus plan isn't reinforcing the appropriate measures, then you haven't picked the right plan, or you haven't picked the right measures. You should be measuring and evaluating how well you're doing every month. If you've got a problem, then it's a call to action—not to beat people up, but to figure out what the problem is and fix it." He adds that it's rarely wise to make change in midcourse. ("That tends to undermine trust.") But at the end of the year, or whenever the bonus period ends, take a good, hard look at it and figure out what needs to be changed.

This reevaluation has to take place along five dimensions.

1. *Do employees understand the plan?* Can they explain exactly what measures drive the bonus, how much they may earn (and when), and how things look on the bonus front this

month or this quarter? A plan that isn't transparent is like no plan at all.

2. *Do they think the plan is fair—and big enough to make a difference?* These are two separate questions, but they're both subjective and thus hard to gauge. People's sense of whether the plan is fair turns on that issue of how big each individual's share is. A generous award can seem small if someone you don't think deserves it gets three times as much. "Big enough to make a difference" depends mightily on employees' perceptions of their own situation and the company's. If they feel they're being well paid *relative to what the company can pay*, the bonus doesn't have to be as big as it might otherwise have to be. If they feel underpaid, or if they think the company's owners are getting rich and aren't sharing it, then they're apt to view the bonus as window dressing.

3. *Are they excited about it?* Bonuses should be fun, stimulating, worth talking about, worth watching. Any plan gets old after a few years—which is why Samuel Smith of Smith & Company Engineers decided to abolish his bucket plan in 1997. It was effective and well understood and generated a good deal of excitement. But Smith felt that after three years of buckets, a new plan would stimulate even more interest.

The measures have to do with employees' perceptions of, and feelings toward, the plan. Two others have to do with whether the plan is effective.

4. *Are the numbers moving in the right direction?* This is the most important gauge for any bonus plan. If it isn't affecting performance, it isn't working. Note that word *performance*, rather than *profit*. A company's profits depend on any number of factors, some of which are beyond employees' (or anyone's) control. Performance on the measures that drive the bonus, however—throughput, billable hours, whatever they may be—should be up.

5. *What does the company need* now? Bonus plans have to change from year to year, simply because companies' needs change. The planning-and-assessment process (see Chapter 11) should help you identify your company's opportunities and vulnerabilities; it should also identify the metrics that need to move

in the right direction if your company is to reach its goals for the year. These are the metrics that should drive the bonus.

Equity and Long-Term Thinking

Many (perhaps most) open-book companies are owned, in whole or in part, by their employees. They have employee stock ownership plans (ESOPs), which hold sizable stakes in the company. If they're publicly traded, they have stock-option and stock-purchase plans. Some of these companies provide a portion of employees' variable compensation each year in the form of stock rather than straight cash.

Equity is the final step in aligning the interests of everyone who works for a company. Without it, there is a built-in tension between the interests of owners, who want to see their equity grow, and employees, who want cash compensation. But equity is more than that. It's a powerful tool to help people think about and plan for the long term. It's a source of wealth beyond what most people can hope to earn from wages or salaries. Owning a stake in a company is what being a businessperson is all about. It's the heart of the free-enterprise system.

Equity teaches what *Inc.* editor-in-chief George Gendron calls "the magic of the multiple." If employees can increase a company's profits by $500,000 in one year, and if the price-to-earnings ratio in that industry is 15, then, others things being equal, they have added $7.5 million to the value of the business. If they own a substantial stake in the business, they stand to realize much more than they could have gained just by sharing the profits. Growth in a capitalist society creates wealth for owners. If employees own a part of their company, they are owners, and they can create wealth—real wealth—for themselves.

Some companies are too small to share ownership easily, and some company owners choose not to share equity for other reasons. Open-book management is still possible, particularly if the owners are willing to establish some sort of long-term bonus or phantom-stock plan. At Cascade Bookkeeping, for instance, the company's small size (ten employees) makes an ESOP impractical. But Cascade distributes a portion of its bonus pool in Phantom Mine certificates, which function much like stock. They are revalued at the end of each year to reflect the change in Cascade's gross annual billings as compared with the prior year. They can't be sold or traded, but the company will redeem them for cash (paid in five annual installments) if an employee leaves.*

---

* For additional information on employee stock plans, contact the National Center for Employee Ownership, 1201 Martin Luther King Jr. Way, Oakland, CA, 94612-1217.

Steal This Bonus!

Or at least borrow what's relevant to your business. Open-book companies have developed some great bonus-design ideas, and there's no need to reinvent the wheel completely. In this chapter you'll find the distinctive features of ten bonus plans. The brief write-ups aren't intended to be comprehensive—that would take up half the book—only to showcase how a few more companies resolved some of the issues discussed in the previous two chapters.

Amoco Canada: Marrying divisional and corporate goals

Amoco Canada's bonus plan during 1996 was pegged half to the performance of Amoco Corporation ("our investor," as one Canadian manager characterized the company) and half to the performance of Amoco Canada itself. Each entity had to hit a target for return on capital employed (ROCE) before it was liable for its share of the bonus. (ROCE is a return-on-assets measure, calculated by taking net income before interest and dividing by long-term debt plus owners equity.)

Once that gate was open, the parent corporation's contribution was pegged to its competitive performance. If it beat the average ROCE of its seven chief competitors, so much went into the bonus pool. If it beat the average of its three top competitors, so much more went in. This portion of the bonus would max out if Amoco Corporation beat them all. Amoco Canada's contribution was pegged to targets for operating income (measured in dollars of net income, not percentages) and replacement of oil and gas reserves (a key measure for any energy company). Goals were set at three levels, with higher payouts at each level.

Bottom line: Amoco Canada employees could make up to 16 percent of their salaries with stellar performance at both the corporate and the divisional levels. If performance was good enough to open the gates, but not quite stellar, they'd make less—as little as a few percent of salary. (As it happened, Amoco Canada's year in 1996 was its best ever, though not quite up to the ambitious level reflected in the targets; the payout was 10.1 percent.)

Amherst Woodworking: More profits = a *lot* bigger bonus

Amherst Woodworking & Supply makes custom cabinetry for commercial and residential customers and runs a small milling operation. The company's plan puts a varying percentage of pretax profits into the bonus pool, with the percentage determined by return on sales (RoS). If RoS is 4 percent or less, there's no bonus. If it's between 4 percent and 5 percent, then 10 percent of total profit dollars goes into the pool. As RoS rises, so does the *percentage* of profit dollars going into the pool. At RoS of 14 percent or above, 30 percent of all profits is distributed as bonuses.

The effect: an improvement in profit margin can bring a disproportionate increase in the size of the bonus. For example, say that pretax profits are $40,000 on sales of $1 million, so RoS is 4 percent. Since 10 percent of profits goes into the pool, the pool is $4,000. If profits hit $60,000, or 6 percent, however, the plan specifies that 14 percent of that profit goes into the pool. Now the pool is $8,400—more than twice as big, even though RoS has risen only by half.

Amherst Woodworking distributes 85 percent of its pool on the basis of W-2 earnings, with managers getting twice as much per dollar of earnings as hourly employees. The other 15 percent is divided on the basis of seniority; an employee with ten years' seniority thus gets ten times as much from this portion of the pool as does a one-year employee.

Mountain Travel Sobek: Targeting the drivers

In 1996, the bonus program at Mountain Travel Sobek, an adventure-travel company, was pegged to net income and gross margin.

But not many employees understood how what they did every day affected those two numbers. In 1997, the company revamped its plan, so that 80 percent of the bonus would depend on net income and 20 percent on departmental goals. Salespeople had to bring in a certain number of passengers. Operations and customer-service folks (the people who design and manage trips) had to hit targets for gross profit per passenger. Marketing was shooting for a certain gross profit per marketing dollar, finance and accounting for a reduction in overhead, and so on.

The idea, explained CFO Jim Ahern, was to target the variables that would drive net income, and the effect was to make MTS's ambitious profit goals for 1997 seem reachable. "Our company-wide goals, they look a little daunting. But when you go into the details, when you look at the departmental goals, they're doable. People say, 'Yeah, I think we can do that.' And if we do, we'll reach the overall goal."

Hexacomb Corporation: Beat the budget

Hexacomb Corporation, a division of Tenneco Packaging, operates seven plants that produce honeycomb, a corrugated-paper material used in a variety of applications. Each plant gets a budget every year, including a goal for operating profit. Every profit dollar beyond that goal is split 50–50, with half going to the company and half into a bonus pool. However, the pool is determined by adding up all seven plants' profits or losses, so any plant that is negative (compared to budget) subtracts from the overall pool. In addition, only employees of plants that beat *their* budgets are eligible for a bonus.

What makes this an effective incentive is that Hexacomb's operations are relatively simple—more production means more profit. Employees see their production and financial-performance figures every week and know that if they're at (or above) 100 percent of budgeted production, the likelihood of a bonus is high.

Critz Inc.: The critical-number plan

Critz Inc., the auto dealer, pegs its bonus directly to its critical number, which shows up at the bottom of its scorecard every month. Critz's critical number depends on three factors. The first is operating profit, which is calculated in the conventional manner. The second is an adjustment for noncash assets on the balance sheet;

this adjustment gives Critz's employees an incentive to manage inventory and receivables tightly. The third is an adjustment for the dealership's customer-satisfaction rating, which is provided by the manufacturer it represents. The higher the rating, the higher the critical number. "Everybody has a matrix for each quarter," explains vice president and general manager Dale Critz Jr. "You just go down one side of it, find the critical number, then read across. You'll find a percentage. That's the percentage of your year-to-date earnings you'll get as a bonus."

If Critz Inc. makes plan, the bonus is worth 10 percent of W-2 earnings. It can rise or fall if the company's performance is better or worse than plan.

Terminix (North Carolina): The current-ratio payout

Terminix of North Carolina, a pest-control business that is a franchise of a national company, sets a sales and profit goal for each of its branches and puts 25 percent of profits over the goal into a bonus pool. Half the bonus is paid quarterly; the other half is paid at the end of the year and is paid only if the branches hit a goal for their current ratio. The reason? "One of the hardest parts of our business is accounts receivable," explains president Harden Blackwell. Each branch had to pay a portion of its profits to the franchisor at the end of every period and often didn't have the cash. "That's when their current ratios went to hell." Blackwell gave his service technicians a quick lesson in the balance sheet—and in the importance of cash. "Now they'll start building their cash up. And as they build their cash up, their current ratio will go up."

Visual In-Seitz: The evolution of four measurements

"We tailor how much each person gets to a set of measurements that we feel determines what they contributed toward us making money," explains Charles (Chad) Engler, president of the Rochester, New York, business-presentation company. The pool is roughly 25 percent of company profits. It's divided up according to four criteria:

1. An equal split. "If I'm measuring productivity, it's going to be harder to measure the receptionist, say, than a production person. So the even split is designed to take care of that discrepancy."

2. Total hours worked. Originally, this accounted for half the bonus. "But if you're rewarding people who work a million hours, they'll work a million hours. People were working crazy hours and making a ton of money. But the company wasn't." So Visual In-Seitz put a ceiling on the amount people could make by working extra hours and added a third measurement.

3. Billable hours as a percentage of total hours worked. "We wanted to have people working 40 hours a week make just as much money as those working 50 or 60—by working smart enough."

4. "We realized we were still missing an element. For every job that comes in here, someone is responsible for it. It's an important job to manage incoming work, and if we don't reward that, people will do something else that gets noticed and rewarded. So that's when we added the last portion: the cumulative profitability of jobs we're responsible for."

Pettit Fine Furniture: Profit sharing with a kicker

Pettit's bonus pool is a percentage of net profit; it cuts in above 7 percent RoS. But the company adds a kicker—a second goal that acts as a multiplier, positive or negative, on the pool. In 1995 the kicker was sales. "We had recently moved to a larger facility, and we had the overhead situation," explains Kim Kenyon, co-owner of the 14-employee company. The focus on sales helped the business grow. In 1996, Kenyon felt that sales were under control, and so changed the kicker. The new one was the ratio of actual hours to projected hours on every job, a critical variable for the boardroom-furniture builder.

If the actual-to-projected ratio is below 1:15, the pool can increase up to 50 percent. If the ratio is above that level, it can shrink by 50 percent. Kenyon said soon after the plan was implemented that the new kicker was having the desired effect. "People are really fixating on the ratio." They were even asking for more information so they could figure out in advance what the ratio needed to be.

RR Donnelley & Sons: Drivers for each business unit

The Northeastern Division of the big printing company—a 2,100-employee complex encompassing four distinct business units—

developed an open-book bonus plan in 1997. Teams of managers and supervisors set goals for each business unit along two different dimensions. ("We wanted to get at the couple of things that really have some ability to influence our numbers," explained OBM project leader Don Robb, "and we wanted them to be things that people touch and handle every day.") In the East Plant print-and-bind operation, for example, the first goal was an improvement of so much percent over the previous year's performance on materials yield (i.e., reducing paper waste). The second was an improvement in throughput. Each goal was translated into dollars. An improvement in paper usage, for example, was calculated as pounds of paper saved times the average price per pound of paper. Performance better than the threshold level thus created a pool of dollars, which became the payout pool for that business unit. Performance worse than the threshold subtracted dollars from the pool.

Donnelley uses economic value added (EVA)—a calculation of profitability that factors in the company's cost of capital—as a measure of business-unit performance. "At the end of every quarter," explains Robb, "the EVA performance of each unit will determine the percentage of the bucket [the profit pool] that is paid out. For example, at the end of the first quarter, anywhere from 5 to 15 percent of the bucket can be paid out. If EVA is on the low end, it'll be 5 percent. If it's on the high end, it'll be 15 percent.

"The payout is 5 to 15 percent the first quarter, 10 to 20 percent the second, 15 to 25 percent the third, and 20 to 30 percent the fourth. So it always escalates, and it's always going to be a cumulative number. At the end of every quarter you take the cumulative amount in the bucket and calculate the year-to-date EVA, which determines the percentage of the bucket that is shared. Then you subtract any prior payments to get that quarter's payout." Thus the company could have three so-so quarters and a great fourth quarter, and employees would still get a nice bonus. (See Chapter 20 for more on Donnelley's bonus plan.)

Share Group: One key goal

In 1996, the bonus at this telephone marketing and fund-raising company was based on companywide profits. In 1997 the plan was organized around the company's six call centers—and around one key driver. Each center's objective: reduce the ratio of labor costs to net revenue. A 1 percentage-point improvement in that ratio (compared to plan) would generate a bonus pool of 1 percent of net revenue. Corporate and staff employees at Share had a similar plan, but it was based on reducing overhead as a percentage of gross profit.

Call-center employees know how to impact the labor-cost ratio: manage their time more efficiently, make more calls per hour, help ensure that lines are fully staffed. "It's a very easy thing for people to figure out and track," says general manager Sue Meehan. "That labor-cost percentage is displayed in our scorecard meetings every week. There's a plan, and the centers project how they'll do, and [the spreadsheet] actually calculates for them what the bonus pool will be if they hit those projections. So they see it on a weekly basis."

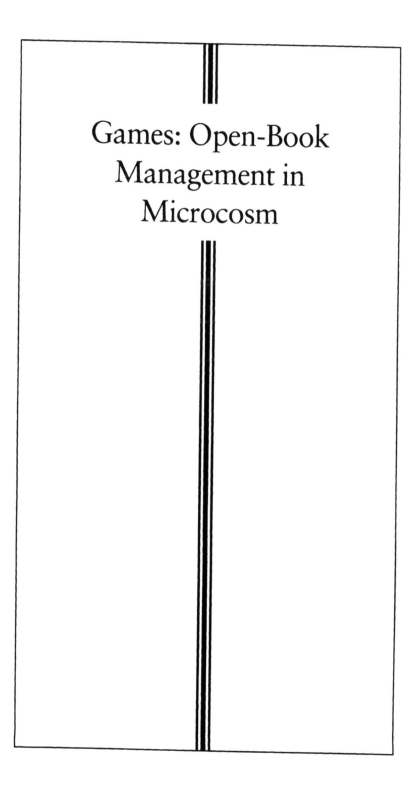

Games: Open-Book Management in Microcosm

Overview: The Meaning of Games

Not long ago, the employees at Dixie Iron Works Inc., in Alice, Texas, were in need of some time off, and operations vice president Gerard Danos figured that the slow period between Christmas and New Year's was a good time to declare a company holiday. But the company had been hitting its monthly shipping targets with great regularity, and Danos didn't want to ruin the record. Besides, if the company could somehow hit its December target by the Friday before Christmas, he realized, it would get a triple windfall. "We'd ship what we wanted to ship anyway. We'd save about a quarter of a large electric bill. And we'd save on payroll because there'd be less overtime pay."

So Danos announced a game: hit the target by that Friday, with no increase in scrap, and everybody would get a paid vacation.

Suddenly everyone at Dixie was working even harder than before. They cranked out the jobs. They checked the scoreboard to see if they were on track. "If I didn't post the previous day's shipping chart by 7:30 A.M.," says Danos, "the *janitors* would ask, 'Hey, how in hell did we do?'" By Christmas, the company had not only met its target, it had set a new monthly shipping record in only three weeks. "All told, we got ten calendar days off, and we saved on payroll and electric. After we closed the books in December, the owner was so amazed he handed out bonuses."

There you have it: a business game.

A *game* is simply a short-term initiative designed to reach a particular goal. It includes a way of tracking progress as the game progresses (a scoreboard). It involves a payoff or reward of some sort at the end. Games are open-book management in microcosm.

They embody open-book principles, but they're circumscribed in time and space. They can last for a week, a month, six months. They can involve a whole company, a business unit, or only one small department. Games are an immensely important part of open-book management. They are also an immensely powerful management tool—a tool, however, that is available only to open-book companies.

This chapter explains how and why games work, and why conventional companies can't use them as open-book companies can. The next chapter is a compendium of real-world games that have helped open-book companies boost their performance.

Games and Business

Game playing bears on that most elusive of managerial and organizational challenges: human motivation.

Professional athletes and serious gamblers aside, people play games for one reason and one reason only: they enjoy the experience. They like learning and testing new skills. They enjoy the camaraderie of a team, or even of competitors (think of golf or poker). They like the competition itself, whether against others or against their own past performances. They like to win. Games are exciting. Games are fun.

Think of business in this context, and you're immediately struck by a paradox.

To a lot of people—venture investors, entrepreneurs, many executives and business owners—business *is* essentially a game. They're players. They know the rules. They enjoy matching wits with the marketplace and with each other. To be sure, there can be substantial rewards for success, but the game itself is often more important than the reward. "The money is just a way of keeping score" is a common refrain among such people, which is one reason they keep playing even when they have more than enough money to retire.

In the lower ranks, however, business is anything but a game. Work is work. You show up, do your job, get your check, go home. The gamelike aspects of business—the thrill of making risky decisions, keeping score, watching the results, testing yourself against the competition—are so well hidden they might as well be nonexistent. And most people get the same reward from one month to the next regardless of how well they do their job or how well their company performs. So the score, in effect, is always the same.

Open-book management cuts through this paradox by teaching everybody in a company to be players. It teaches them the rules of business, how to keep score, and how to participate in making decisions that will affect the score one way or another. It lets them share in the rewards of winning. Jack Stack called his pioneering open-book system The Great Game of Business for just this reason. Open-book management is a way of making business more enjoyable, of making work more like play. It spreads the extrinsic rewards around, yes—but you can do that with a plain profit-sharing or stock-ownership plan. What open-book management really does is build up the intrinsic rewards of working.

Game playing—setting out to achieve a short-term goal, figuring out how you're going to get there, watching the scoreboard to see what's effective and what's ineffective—takes the open-book system and makes it a part of people's daily lives on the job. It brings a little excitement and a little challenge to the workplace. Set up a game and something quite amazing happens. Suddenly people aren't just doing their jobs, they're working for a purpose. They *want* to make that goal. They want to win. They bring the same interest, intensity, and desire that they bring to volleyball or bridge or their kids' soccer games. They don't need to be motivated, because they motivate themselves and each other.

Conventional companies can rarely tap this power. Oh, maybe they can do it now and then; they can mount a big push to get past a production crunch, for example, or they can set up a challenge to get a new product out the door. Continental Airlines at one point wanted to improve its on-time performance, so it put up monitors showing employees the daily on-time percentages and promised a small bonus for each month the airline scored high in the government's on-time rankings. Employees in conventional companies will play games like this once, twice, even three times. (Continental's performance did indeed improve.) But the game playing gets old fast. If you never see what all that hoopla and hard work mean to the success of the business, you never really know if you've won or lost. If you're not sharing in the rewards, you eventually feel like a drone, not like a player. After a few such games, the other meaning of *games* cuts in: "They're playing games with us." Once that happens, attempts at game playing merely boost the level of cynicism.

Open-book companies can utilize games precisely because they teach the "big game"—business—and make it plain how all the little games tie into the big one. Small games are fun and interesting, but they also make the business stronger in ways people learn to understand. Because everyone has an interest in a stronger business, everyone has an interest in winning the game.

How Games Strengthen a Company (and OBM)

Eliminating business problems

"Whenever you identify a problem," says Steve Wilson, founder of Mid-States Technical, "create a game to solve it." Mid-States Technical's problem at one point was inaccurate time sheets, which were screwing up the company's payroll; only 62 percent of all time sheets were free of errors. So one of Wilson's people designed a game: teams of employees would take responsibility for batches of time sheets and would play to see who could record the fewest mistakes. In three weeks, says Wilson, the time sheets were 100 percent accurate. The game went on for 10 weeks, however, just to make sure people got in the habit of checking and rechecking the sheets. At the end of the year accuracy was at 99.6 percent.

How do conventional companies attack business problems like these? They issue memos and instructions. They exhort the troops, threaten, cajole. Games, in contrast, capture the intrinsic reward of meeting a challenge. They're leavened by the zest of competition, whether it's among teams (as in Mid-States' case) or purely against the problem. They can also be applied in nearly any situation. Your quality isn't what it should be? Your inventory has been climbing faster than sales? Your people aren't up to speed on the new software? Your freight costs are out of line? Set up a game, target an objective—and watch things happen.

Helping to deal with everyday challenges

Some aspects of running a business are tedious. They can't be avoided, but they don't get anybody's juices flowing. An example is the problem of maintaining safety in an industrial plant. No worker wants to be injured in an accident. Most managers understand that a good safety record is in everyone's interest. Still, stuff happens. Guards are left off machines. Hazardous chemicals are handled carelessly. Aisles get blocked, hoists go uninspected, forklifts don't get their preventive-maintenance checks. Management's response, typically, is to put up more safety posters, send more people off to training classes, carry out more surprise inspections—and hope to heaven that nothing happens.

Compare that traditional approach with a game-oriented approach such as that of Springfield ReManufacturing's Heavy-Duty Division:

- Heavy-Duty employees without a recordable accident in the previous month can enter a drawing for a $10 bill; six winners are picked every week.

- Workers who submit suggestions for safety improvements can win up to $50. The plant's 12-member safety committee gets about a dozen suggestions each month.

- A safety-awareness week held one fall featured a free lunch, all-day bingo, a safety-slogan contest, and gift certificates at the local Wal-Mart.

- In June 1996, the company received its official induction into OSHA's Voluntary Protection Program, an elite group of 200-plus companies that pass a rigorous application and inspection process and are then entrusted with monitoring their own safety. SRC celebrated with a 24-hour party, with T-shirts, food, awards, and more gift certificates (including ten weekend-getaway prizes worth $500 apiece).

SRC also does all the conventional things—training, instruction, inspections. But the games help keep things lively (and keep people's eyes from glazing over). The problem of maintaining safety is no longer only management's concern, it's everyone's; and solving the problem isn't just one more burden to worry about, it's an opportunity to participate and have some fun.

Building a culture of fun

Many of the best companies are known as great places to work—often because working there isn't just a chore, it's a chance to have a good time while you're making money. Southwest Airlines' flight attendants have been known to hide in overhead compartments as passengers board the plane. AGI Inc. chief executive Richard Block encourages employees to ask him tough questions at the company's monthly meetings—and then may literally stand on his head while he answers them. Games show people it's okay to have fun, even at less-nutty companies. The staff of Mountain Travel Sobek worked together to hit certain sales targets and received bottles of wine if they were successful. Cornwell, Jackson & Company, an accounting and financial-services firm in Dallas, divided its employees into two teams, set up a game to encourage referrals and new accounts, and described the award for the winning team as follows:

> The winners will receive a dinner or lunch prepared and served by the losing team. The firm will provide the food, the losers will provide the sweat, blood, and tears. Only after the winners have been suitably served and their appetites satiated, will the losing team be afforded the opportunity to dine . . . . this in addition to bragging rights, which will not be insignificant.

And this in an accounting firm!

Teaching open-book management

What happens in a business game? People decide on an objective. They brainstorm ways to reach it. They learn how to monitor their progress, and they get a reward if they reach the goal. But this simple synopsis glosses over what may be a significant learning experience for employees. Just to play the game, people have to ask themselves any number of questions. What are reasonable objectives for our department? Are there ways of reorganizing the work so as to reach those objectives faster or more efficiently? What are the best metrics to use—and how can we make sure everybody sees them and understands them? Is this initiative likely to have any unintended effects? Learning the answers to such questions means learning open-book management. People come to see that work isn't a disembodied series of tasks, it's effort that is coordinated and directed toward a goal—as in a game.

Doing It Right

Open-book companies have learned plenty of lessons about successful game playing. For example:

Games work best when they're created by the people who will be playing them. That doesn't mean managers should sit back and do nothing. Managers are often the first to spot problems. They may have ideas about a good game for addressing the problem. But games that are imposed from above can encounter the same problems as games in a conventional company: yawns, sighs, eyes rolled skyward, foot dragging. Better to convene a committee and say, Here's the problem—anybody have ideas for a game to solve it?

Games have to be tailored to the players. Young, male warehouse workers and older, female office employees have different ideas of fun. Gregarious salespeople feel comfortable doing things that reclusive computer programmers would hate. To a certain extent, games can pull people out of their shells and get them to take part in group activities, even if they feel a little uncomfortable at first. But there's no point in a game with football terminology among people who don't like football, and there's no point at all in a game that seems somehow cutesy, strained, or manipulative. Again, get the players involved in designing the game. You reduce the risks it will misfire.

Games are played mainly against the problem, not against each other. Even companies that set up competitive teams know this: typically, the prize for reaching the goal, which everybody gets, is more significant than the prize for winning the competition, which only the winners get. Competition can be fun so long as it doesn't overshadow the common goal, which is to strengthen the company.

A corollary: rewards should go to everyone, not just to a few. The worst games have one or two winners and a lot of losers. The best ones reward all the players for their collective accomplishment—with small cash bonuses, a free lunch, gift certificates, whatever. The occasional game of chance, as at SRC, never hurts, but it shouldn't overshadow the group's achievements, and the group's rewards.

But rewards should be small. When people play a game outside work, they rarely expect any reward. Business games are no different: the real reward is in playing, not in what you get. The reward, typically, is simply a celebration of success. People get a few bucks or a free lunch. It's not the *reason* for the extra effort, it's just a way by which the players can pat themselves on the back for putting out the extra effort.

Be sure your games make good business sense. One company played a game to boost its on-time delivery from below 90 to 96 percent—and the percentage did indeed increase, to nearly 96 percent. But achieving the goal meant that production runs were being interrupted, the company was paying extra for overnight freight, and costs were rising on several other fronts. The conclusion? The result wasn't worth the extra expense. "In our industry, 90 percent on time is fine, so long as we're keeping the other 10 percent of our customers informed," says the manager in charge.

Games have to be coordinated among a company's departments.
RR Donnelley & Sons Company's Northeastern Division established a small games council, charged, among other chores, with establishing divisionwide guidelines for games. At another company that launched open-book management, some departments began playing games while others didn't. "That was a big problem," reports a manager. Some people were getting rewards while others were not—and some of the rewards were tokens, such as a pizza lunch, while others were sizable cash bonuses.

Games have to be integrated with the rest of open-book management. What does the goal of a game—reducing a department's office-supplies expense, for instance—have to do with the company's business objectives? How does it relate to the critical numbers, or to the business unit's financial performance? If those connections aren't clear, game playing will soon come to seem like an idle exercise. If the connections are clear, however, then game playing is meaningful within the whole open-book context. It helps build a stronger company. It increases the likelihood that there will be wealth—real wealth—to be shared. It increases the likelihood that open-book management will work.

**CHAPTER
FIFTEEN**

Steal This Game!

Open-book companies use games for all kinds of purposes: to boost sales, reduce costs, improve quality, you name it. Figure out the problems in your business—and then see if there isn't a game in this compendium that you can adapt.

Reducing Postage Costs

Suzanne Kreitzberg, consultant to Colburn-Bertholon-Rowland (Media, Pa.): "This company is an insurance agency and brokerage with 135 employees. Postage costs for marketing, billing, and administration run $10,000 to $12,000 a month. The Games Committee's first goal was to cut those costs. Half of every dollar saved over budget would go into a bonus pool, to be distributed at the end of the quarter, and half would go back to the company. The committee wanted to focus attention on *how* things were mailed, not necessarily on what was mailed. Could some packages go out on two-day rather than overnight delivery? Could the company utilize zip-plus-four, bar coding, or any other money-saving techniques?

"They kept score on a thermometer, with weekly numbers supplied by the mail room and accounting, and on the financials every month. At the end of a quarter, they had saved $9,000."

Meeting Sales Goals

Jennifer Pearl, managing partner, Bagel Works Inc. (Keene, N.H.): "We have little games in every store. There's the weekly game for meeting sales objectives: everybody gets a lottery ticket. We've done suggestive selling, where if you can get someone to upgrade from plain cream cheese to a veggie cream cheese, you get a check—and a certain number of checks wins that week's game. We've also done things like try to move a certain number of people through the lines within an hour. If they do that, they get an award—sometimes cash, sometimes a free lunch, sometimes just the incentive of winning the game. In the production facility, people have done a real good job of coming up with games. How quickly can they break down a machine and get it cleaned? How quickly can they box bagels? What's the total cost of boxing bagels? That kind of thing."

Competing for Profits

John DeMaine, Carolina Safety Associates (Gastonia, N.C.): "Right now we have a baseball game going. Each of our 13 branches is a team, and then there are a couple of teams composed of people from our internal service groups, the people who service all our branches. We'll have a four-month regular season starting in April, then play-offs in September and the World Series in October. During the season, each team plays another team according to a predetermined schedule. You get so many runs for exceeding your sales goals, and so many more for exceeding your gross-profit and net-profit targets. There are prizes every month for the team with the most runs and the best record. Ultimately, we'll pass out $15,000 to the winning team, with smaller cash awards for second and third place. So far, everybody's pumped about it. Also, it's the first time we've had a company-wide game where the service groups participated, and it has given these groups some identity that they didn't have before."

Boosting Cross-Selling and Referrals

Gary Jackson, principal, Cornwell, Jackson & Company, (Dallas): "The biggest game we have going on right now is the Green versus White game. We split the firm into two teams, Green and White. Those are the firm's colors. The purpose is to capitalize on cross-selling opportunities. We offer a variety of different services—consulting, accounting, technology, and financial-planning services. We wanted to get professionals in one service discipline aware of opportunities for us to provide other services. That would not only increase our overall revenues, it would help knock down the silos that each group tends to work in.

"In the game, each team gets a certain number of points for referring different kinds of clients, existing or new. You get one point if you send a warm referral to somebody. You get two points if you make an introduction, on the phone or in person. You get three additional points if that referral turns into billables. The losers cook and serve dinner for the winning team. But if the company as a whole scores more than 300 points by April 15, we'll all take a day off and go to Six Flags, at the company's expense."

Better Time-Entry Compliance

Larry Cone, founder and CEO, Cone Software (Boothwyn, Pa.): "We missed our bonus goals the first two quarters of this year, so we began working on our problems. One thing we didn't always have was good, up-to-date information on how people were spending their time and what was being billed. So we developed a sort of minigame to encourage daily time entry into our time system. Here's how it works. Every day, one of our administrative people runs a report showing the percentage of time-entry compliance to date. That goes out on E-mail, including the names and percentages of the 'offenders.' We started out saying that if we got over 90 percent compliance, we'd have a company lunch—and we did. Now we've raised the bar, and we're targeting 95 percent for the next lunch."

Lowering Errors (and Finger-Pointing)

Michael Crisp, president, Crisp Publications (Menlo Park, Calif.): "In our Crisp Fulfillment Center, we have two distinct groups. One is customer service, which takes the order and creates the invoice. The other is the warehouse, which ships the materials. There was always a lot of finger-pointing between the two. The warehouse would say that customer service didn't write up the order correctly. Customer service would say warehouse pulled the wrong book. It was never a huge problem—our error rate was 0.6 percent, which is about six shipments out of 1,000. But no one was incentivized to solve it.

"Anyway, we started the game by saying, 'Look, it's not *you* and *me*, it's *us*. And we promised to give everybody $30 a month extra if they got the error rate below 0.5%. Well, the error rate improved immediately. It dipped below 0.5 percent and stayed there for the following four or five months. Then we asked them if they'd be interested in shooting for 0.3 percent, which is about what they were hitting. They said yeah, and we upped the incentive to $40 a month. Eventually we upped it to $50 and set the goal at 0.2 percent. Some months they hit it, some months they don't. But they're always close."

Increasing Average Sale per Customer

A manager at a West Coast retail chain: "To develop monthly games, I get a group together of employees and general managers and say, 'What can we do now? This is what our financial statement looks like, this is where we are to date, how can we improve these areas?' The monthly games change depending on the area we're working on. Most of them focus on sales: customer count, average sale per customer. Right now we're handing out lottery tickets every time we beat average sale per customer in every store. We've also done silver dollars—we ordered them from the Federal Reserve. Employees know what their average sale per customer was last year. They can do register readings as often as they want to find out what it is today. We've done that game twice because it seemed to generate a lot of excitement.

"Another game is derived from the bonus plan. We're trying to have a 15 percent increase in sales in order to pay employees a certain level of bonus. So each store figured out what their goal was: 'This is how much we have to do every single day in order to beat our goal for the month.' Then we break it out on a daily basis, and we have a big chart so every day they have to either do, you know, $6,000, $10,000, whatever. And every day they beat it they got a silver dollar or a lottery ticket or a Baskin-Robbins coupon. We try to keep it nominal so we don't have to report it."

Starting Work on Time

Julie Lotesto, operations manager, Glavin Security Hardware Specialists (Chicago): "We had a big problem getting people in here on time. That's the nature of this business—service technicians are highly skilled people, and they seem to come in when they want to! So the employees came up with an idea. If people got here by 7:00 A.M. every day for a month, they'd get two 'well hours.' Two extra hours off, paid by the company. They could use them however they wanted to: save them up, take two hours off on a Monday, whatever. Or save them up until the end of the year, and get the whole thing in a cash bonus. It worked really well. On-time attendance improved by almost 85 percent."

Making Better Estimates

Ron Stewart, president, Heflin Steel Company (Phoenix): "We're trying to improve our estimating abilities. So we're having a game this month where everybody gets to guess what they think our gross margin is going to be for the month. We tell them what the salesmen have predicted before the first of the year and what they're predicting for this month, and we're giving a little incentive on it. A dinner for two, or a night out. Actually, the game is slightly different for different people. For the salespeople, it's how close can they come to their own number. The shop people, the operations people, who might not be as close to the estimating process, they'll get a special prize for whoever's closest. At the end of the first week our general manager was the closest. After the second week the purchasing manager was in the lead, with one of the fellows in the shop very close to him. But that's just based on our projections. It's like a horse race—you get it going and then when we get to the home stretch we might post it on a day-to-day basis. Then we'll find out who really won at the end of the month."

Getting the Tedious Work Done

Dale Hoffmann, vice president, operations, Jim's Formal Wear (Trenton, Ill.): "One of our regional centers developed what we call the Teardown game. Teardowns are the physical act of taking a returned tux and breaking it into its different parts and throwing them in the right bins. Before, people had to be pretty much drafted to go back there and do teardowns. They wanted to give themselves an incentive to do the job and to get it done early. So we decided, if we can get all the teardowns done by 11:30 A.M. every day for a month, we'd provide a catered lunch. Anything they want—Chinese food, barbecued ribs, whatever.

"I figured this was a nice game, but it didn't really affect profits. Then I was talking to a customer-service rep who mentioned what a great game it was. I asked her why. She said, 'Oh, it does affect profits. Because they get those teardowns done faster, I can run a printout of outstanding garments and can make the calls much earlier in the day to people who didn't return them. And that's much more effective.'"

Improving Quality Levels

Frank Topinka, president, McKenna Professional Imaging (Waterloo, Iowa): "Our customers are portrait or wedding photographers, so every order that comes into our facility is a custom order. Our customers are naturally very demanding. So we're asking ourselves what we can do to get our level of quality higher.

"We started out by monitoring remakes. Those are the external failures—the job actually comes back to you. We paid $15 per person for every month that we were below 1.5 percent, and we were able to drive the number down to where we wanted it. Then we attacked rework, which is internal failures. You catch the error before it goes out the door. We audit our jobs, two for every 12 orders, and rank them as pass, marginal, or fail. Pass is green, marginal is yellow, and fail is red. If you get one red or two yellows, that's a failure. Then you calculate the auditing interval until the next failure, and change the interval according to a formula. The more frequent a failure, the more you have to audit.

"Anyway, you measure the number of errors relative to the error opportunity, which is the number of orders times the number of possible errors we check for. That gives you a performance number. Once we get that number, we say, 'Okay, here it is, let's beat it next time.' And if we do, we'll pass out $15 per person.

"After some time, the performance number was greatly improved. So then we put the incentive on the audit itself, not on the error ratio. We measured how many orders we audit that are not right. If we get 70 percent right one month, then all we have to do the next month is beat that number to get the incentive."

Increasing Cash from Operations

Holly Smith-Bove, financial manager, Motherwear Inc. (Northampton, Mass.): "In the game we played for the last five months, we had two goals: $143,000 in pretax profit, and inventory reduction of $57,000. So that's really a cash-from-operations goal of $200,000. We did a really good job on both goals. We cut our expenses—for example, by learning to handle a larger number of sales calls with the same number of people. At the same time, we were doing target marketing a lot better than before and eliminating less profitable products from our catalog. We also did a big mailing—a clearance flyer—to reduce our inventory. The marketing department worked really hard, the merchandising people did too. Everybody invested a lot into making this happen!"

More-Accurate Information Entry

Richard Weiss, president, Mountain Travel Sobek (El Cerrito, Calif.): "One game we play is this. We get something like 100 catalog requests in a day, and every one has to be entered into the computer system. One thing that makes it easier is if people use standardized abbreviations and forms—the same number of lines for an address, the same location for the apartment number, that sort of thing. Every day we get a printout—and if we have a perfect day I buy lunch. 'Perfect' means *perfect*. We can't have apt. for apartment. It can't be on the line below, it has to be on the same line as the street address. All the states and provinces have to be done correctly. If there's one mistake, I don't buy lunch."

Getting the Reports Done

David Robbins, accounting-systems specialist, Omega Point Labs (Elmendorf, Tex.): "We're a full-service fire-testing laboratory. And a lot of our customers want the results of our test faxed to them. 'Did we pass or fail? Give me the numbers.' So we fax them the results. Here was your smoke number, here was your flame-spread number, etc. Once you fax that to them, they're happy. And so the attitude becomes, 'Well, I'll get the full report out the door later.' Trouble is, later never comes until the end of the month. By then, I'm going, 'Hey, I need your billings memo *now*.' And they haven't done it yet. It creates a horrible problem for cash flow—and the customer isn't real pleased to get the full report a month later.

"So now, each engineer has five file holders, one for each day of the week, out by the back door. When an engineer's assistant faxes the results to the customer, the assistant puts that fax transmittal sheet in one of the holders. On Friday, the Monday-through-Wednesday boxes can contain only one sheet each. That's what they're allowed, one fax transmittal, because when they generate the report they can take the transmittal out. So the idea is, don't let them accumulate. If they hit the standards, the boss will take them out to lunch."

Increasing Point-of-Sale Accuracy (and Other Goals)

Peggy Wynne Borgman, Preston Wynne Inc. (Saratoga, Calif.): "Our accounting department was wasting all kinds of time cleaning up transactions that were riddled with errors. We were literally running up and down the stairs between our office and the front desk, 'interviewing' the staff members who had performed the transactions. It was driving our controller nuts. So we created Immaculate Transactions, a point-of-sale accuracy game. The team had to maintain an average accuracy rating of 96 percent for two consecutive weeks. If they did, they'd get a $50 cash bonus.

"They managed to do it after about a month of trying. Now they have to maintain that same level while playing the next game, which is designed to improve appointment-scheduling accuracy. We call it Scheduling Excellence. They need a 99 percent accuracy rating for two consecutive weeks to get their prize—then they have to maintain that stat while doing the next game. That will be designed to encourage them to actively 'convert' new guests to regular clients by scheduling another appointment for them.

"Once they understand what it takes to make those stats, the behavior becomes habitual. It's no more of an effort than the way they worked in the past, because they're not having their day interrupted by the accountant, playing Columbo. They know that, for instance, they might need to get on the phone with the morning concierge to get a question answered before they close for the night. In the past, the question would have gone unanswered until the accountant began his investigation. Dropping a ticket into the 'finished' work box when there's a known error on it is now taboo, when before it was reflexive ('Oh, he can figure it out.')."

Increasing Machine Efficiency

Jim Burrows, production supervisor, gravure pressroom, RR Donnelley & Sons Company (Lancaster, Pa.): "Our first game was March through May of 1996. The goal was to increase press efficiency—a measure of throughput that incorporates quality—by 3 percent over 1995's performance. If we hit the goal, we'd save about $26,000 in costs. Just setting up the game had a big effect. Let's say that the schedule allowed eight hours for makeready on a job. In the past, the press crews felt that as long as they were

STEAL THIS GAME!

done in eight hours, they had done a good job. Now they began thinking about ways to do it faster—by bringing out the cylinders ahead of time, for example. People also came to understand the importance of press speed. If they run the press at 25,000 impressions an hour, maybe they can get the job done on schedule. If they figure out how to bump that up to 30,000 impressions an hour, they can cut hours off the job. That creates extra capacity for us, and it allows us to get started on the next job that much sooner."

The All-Company, Better-Your-Numbers Game

William Dee Pickens, founder, Pool Covers Inc. (Richmond, Calif.): "We split the company into three teams—the sales team, the office staff, and the field staff—and assigned $800 in potential bonus to each team. The teams had to come up with individual goals that would improve the company's numbers, and then make those goals over a quarter. The sales team wanted to achieve a healthy increase in sales dollars. The field staff's goal was to increase the percentage of billable time they spent in our customers' backyards. The office people's goal was to get the field staff in the backyard without errors. That means things like giving them the correct address on the correct day the first time, and knowing not to schedule a field person's time so tightly that he or she can't get to the next location on time. We played this game in the last quarter of the year—and everybody made their goals. So we split up the $2,400 equally."

Capturing Keycodes

Kim Ferguson, president, Professional Training International (Orem, Utah): "We're a seminar company, and we market our seminars largely by direct mail. The labels on the brochures we mail out contain a keycode, which tells us which of the many mailing lists we rent that particular individual came from. It's important that we track these keycodes. They help us make more intelligent list decisions, which in turn affects our biggest critical number, response rate.

"Our keycode capture rate for one six-month period averaged 86 percent, pretty good by industry standards, but one month was as low as 83 percent. When we started the Keycode game our goal was a 90 percent capture rate—but if we reached it for four consecutive weeks, the goal would go up by half a percentage point, maxing out at 95 percent. Hitting the goal each week would entitle the employees of the registration department to a series of prizes— mostly small cash awards, but sometimes dinner for two or even a paid day off.

"Once we started the game, our capture rate went up immediately. For the past six weeks it has been 92.7 percent."

Reducing Shop-Supply Expense

Lynn Thompson, president, Thompson Pontiac GMC Cadillac (Springfield, Mo.): "We do different things in different departments. For instance, in our service department, the cost of supplies was running at 3.8 percent of gross revenue. The average dealer was at 2.3 percent. So my service coordinator went to the service technicians and said, 'If we can get our supplies expense below 2 percent, you guys get every dollar we save.' All of the sudden it dropped to 1.3 percent. They're using up every can of WD-40 before they throw it away! They went on a mission, and they did it. Now what we do is, if they keep it under 2 percent, we pay for the insurance on their tools."

The Scoreboard Game

Sarah Montgomery, operations vice president, Woodpro Cabinetry (Cabool, Mo.): "Every quarter, our production teams get money put into their team celebration fund. The dollar amount is based on all the numbers we've been tracking: productivity, reject costs, people costs, safety record. At first we set it up so there were penalties; if reject costs went up, for example, they got money taken out of the fund. But we changed that to reward the right outcome. We want to make sure they're bonused for big productivity increases even if reject costs go up a little. The amounts we pay are per member, so a ten-person team is on an equal footing with a five-person team.

"After nearly a year of play, some teams have more than $300 in their accounts. Most have had some kind of celebration. Some are saving up for jackets with our logo. In short, things seem to be working well—and we're on track for a profitable year."

Encouraging Cross-Training

Dale Hoffmann, vice president, operations, Jim's Formal Wear (Trenton, Ill.): "Our next game was a cross-training game. We said between now and the annual Christmas party, which is held about a week before Christmas, for every three hours you spend training in a department other than your own, you'll get a ticket. And for every time someone walks into your department to train for a few hours, that department's going to get a ticket. And at the Christmas party, we're going to draw a grand prize of a 35-inch color TV for the individual. For the department, we'll draw another ticket and everyone in that department gets a 13-inch color TV. There'll be a host of other, smaller prizes, too.

"We didn't know what to expect when we introduced this game. We had no idea how many people would just look down their noses at it. But every department maxed out their number of training spots—about 20 people—within a day. The exception was our cleaners. There weren't as many people who actually wanted to go back there and learn that job. So they went out and solicited. They really sold themselves. So far they're up to 12 people who'll eventually do some training with them.

"We know a cross-training game like this may be a bit disruptive at times. We've got people who are customer-service stars that are back there hemming pants. But the whole idea is that the more cross-trained they are, the more jobs they can do. That gives us more flexibility as a management staff. And flexibility is critical to us."

Sales Incentives—for Everyone

Phil Hindmarch, operations manager, Ten Thousand Waves (Santa Fe, N.Mex.): "We're a full-service health spa. We had a really successful side game that related to memberships for massage therapy. At the time, we were about to move to our high-season prices. So we decided to offer a discount membership at the low-season prices. People could save about 25 percent by buying these memberships. We set a sales goal of about $4,000 in the last ten days of our low season. And we ended up with about $10,000 in sales. People just jumped on it because they felt they were giving customers a valuable service. Our people don't normally get any sales incentive—we're on a single bonus system, with everybody on the same formula. But we put the word out to everyone that they were really doing the customer a service.

"There was no specific payout. We put all the money for bonuses into the large pool, and quarterly payouts are based on net profit. So we figured that every side game we design increases that larger pool. But we have other fun rewards. I believe the reward for blowing away that $4,000 goal was a watermelon seed spitting contest. We got a bunch of watermelons, and we had a contest to see who could spit the seeds the furthest. The winner got a $25 gift certificate to a local restaurant."

Getting Started: Three Exhibition Games

You can play a game even before you launch open-book management; in fact, it's a good way to get started, provided you're ready to follow through on the next steps. Here is how three companies got the ball rolling.

Lynn Topic, general manager, Dolphin Quest (Mesa, Ariz.): "We have interactive programs in Hawaii and elsewhere, where people actually get in the water and touch dolphins and learn about them. We also run retail stores, and we sell photos and videos of the program. We started with just one department—the video department—because it wasn't breaking even. Average sales per day had been decreasing over the years instead of increasing.

"So we decided to play a game. We had a meeting and brainstormed ways to increase video sales. We said, 'Let's develop a chart and a football field.' If you reached your daily sales goal, you moved along the football field, gaining yardage. You're trying to score a touchdown. And depending on how many touchdowns you score, you get an incentive. We asked people what types of incentives they'd like. We started out with gift certificates, movie tickets, gas coupons, anything. All the ideas came from the staff. Anyway, we played that game for three months and saw a phenomenal increase in sales. We went from 13 videos per day to 17 per day over the next month. That was the difference between our breakeven and losing money."

Kim Kenyon, president, Pettit Fine Furniture (Sarasota, Fla.): "Baseball has spring training; football has its exhibition games. We said, 'Before we get started on the Great Game of Business, let's play an exhibition game. Let's identify the numbers and areas that could better our company.' We chose the problem of lateness, because we had our share of stragglers. Every week in which lateness fell below a certain target, employees earned a small bonus. It was simply success or failure. One person could blow it for the entire company. And it was cumulative; it grew during the eight-week program.

"After the third or fourth week, they were actually losing the exhibition game. Believe me, the people responsible heard about it. As we posted the numbers from week to week, the pressure mounted. The feeling became, We have to perform as a group. People were hearing from each other, 'Hey, set your alarm! Get up earlier!' At the end, we won. We had a pizza party in the factory to pass out the bonuses."

Pat Ekdahl, chief operating officer, Columbia Regional Medical Center Southwest Florida (Ft. Myers, Fla.): "We started by selecting and meeting with a pilot group of 14 people, including myself and the CFO, the directors of our six operative areas, and representatives from each area. Some 60 percent of our hospital's business passes through the operating rooms. We proposed to this pilot group that in lieu of the traditional annual merit increase, we would pay a bonus if a given month's volume in an area was 8 percent better than last year's at the same time. It would go up stepwise; if all six areas hit the goal, the bonus would be bigger.

"The pilot group raised a lot of questions. They also made some good suggestions, such as getting someone from marketing on board and making some cosmetic changes, like paint. Then we rolled it out to all six departments, about 220 employees in all. First we developed a draft document explaining the plan. This was distributed to all 220 employees by members of the pilot group. Then the CFO and I met with groups of 12 to 15 people to answer questions. At the end of each session, I passed out a piece of paper and asked them to write down whether the idea made sense. Nearly everyone said it did.

"At the end of six months, nearly all of the groups had hit their goal and were paid a total of $146,198 in bonuses, versus $99,880 of traditional merit increases. So the total cost of the pilot program was $46,318—but the six-month impact on the hospital's bottom line was $673,036. We also noticed a marked change in behavior. The rooms were turning over faster. People were following up with patients to make sure they were satisfied. One doctor even told me, 'Some of the O.R. personnel came up to me and said, Dr. G—, we've noticed that you aren't bringing a lot of your patients to us. Why is that? What can we do so you'll bring more of your patients to us?' "

Implementing
Open-Book
Management

Overview: The Change Process

"Nobody likes change." What a cliché. My theory is that this shopworn aphorism was dreamed up by a consultant who had spent too many years trying to move some hidebound company off square one. People regard change with all the different attitudes of which human beings are capable. Some view it with fear and loathing. Others figure that a change is a chance to learn something new—or at least an antidote to boredom.

As with individuals, so with organizations. Some companies change easily. Change is part of their culture. The people in the company have been selected (or have selected themselves) for their willingness to change. They've grown accustomed to it. Other companies change only with horrendous difficulty. They have set ways of doing things, long-entrenched patterns of behavior. Their culture values stability, seniority, order. In those companies, most of the people who welcome change have long since departed for more turbulent and exciting environs.

Easy or hard, any change process runs into certain predictable obstacles. For one thing, the people who are reluctant to adapt, however many, drag their feet. People whose interests are threatened—those whose jobs may disappear, for example—erect any obstacle they can in the path of the change bandwagon. In large companies, organizational politics intrudes. Local units fight changes imposed by corporate offices. Corporate reacts defensively when the locals institute changes of their own. If the company is unionized, everybody worries about what the union will do.

These days, moreover, change initiatives run smack into the Dilbert phenomenon. Once, corporate managers could announce an initiative and expect that most people would at least give it the benefit of the doubt. Today, after 15 years of managerial fads and buzzwords, about the best reactions they can expect are snickers around the watercooler and a rash of Dilbert cartoons tacked anonymously on bulletin boards.

So the first questions to ask yourself as you plan the implementation of open-book management are simple. What else have you done recently? And how does open-book fit (or not fit) with it?

Maybe, for example, open-book management is merely the latest in a long line of initiatives that were launched with enormous fanfare and then quietly died out. If that's the case, you have a rather large barrier of skepticism to overcome. The answer to that skepticism is *not* to try to persuade employees that now, really, this is *it*, no, *really*, this is what will make the difference. The answer is to start implementing open-book management and stick with it. *That and nothing else* will persuade them that open-book management is for real.

Or maybe your company has successfully implemented an approach such as total quality management, so that it's now an accepted part of the culture. In that case, the natural first question about open-book management will be, How does this fit with TQM? Are we supposed to forget everything we were taught? TQM and open-book management are complementary, of course, not contradictory. But helping people learn that will take time and effort.

In general, nearly all the managerial tools and techniques introduced during the past 15 years focus on the *how* of a business's operation. They restructure the work (reengineering, lean thinking). They teach employees new skills (TQM) or ask them to cooperate in new ways (self-managing teams). Open-book management focuses on the *why*, the logic of the business. It teaches people what the company is all about, how to track its performance (and their own), how to hold colleagues and coworkers accountable for what they say they're going to do. Any of the how-to techniques can be applied within the open-book context, *if* people think that those techniques will help them reach their business objectives.

Obstacles Peculiar to OBM

So some of the obstacles a company faces in implementing open-book management are similar to those it would face in implementing any change. But some of the obstacles are endemic to the open-book philosophy itself. I count four.

Open-book management is a new way of thinking, not just a new way of doing things. It asks people at all levels of an organization to change patterns of thought that they—and nearly everybody else in an industrial society—assume to be perfectly natural. This is a whole lot harder than asking them simply to undertake new tasks.

Consider what's involved. The practice of hiring large numbers of employees to work under close supervision in an office, store, or factory is only a century or so old. But a century in human affairs might as well be forever. Most of us take it for granted that an employee's job is to do what he or she is told or whatever's in the job description. We have little training in, and therefore little understanding of, how a business operates. We assume that so long as we come in every day and work hard, we're *entitled* to a paycheck at the end of the week and a raise at the end of the year.

Open-book management says, Forget that entitlement. Don't think like an employee, think like a businessperson. Open-book management teaches people how the company operates. It tells them that they are responsible for the contribution of their department or work team to overall performance. Open-book companies are happy to pay good bonuses if the business is doing well, but they pay nothing extra (and usually no raises) if the company has come on hard times. This is not an easy idea for a lot of people to accept (to put it mildly!).

Nor is it easy for many people to accept that their job description no longer encompasses everything that's expected of them. In an open-book company, people are responsible for their job—*and* they're responsible for understanding how the business works, *and* they're responsible for overseeing and improving the performance of their unit. This can be a lot to ask. People need time to get used to the new expectations. Some never will.

Not everyone will respond positively to a bottom-line emphasis. Think about what people in a conventional company worry about and what they're usually judged by. Salespeople concern themselves with top-line revenue. Engineers care about the technical elegance of their work. Marketers focus on market share, QA professionals on quality levels, manufacturing managers on output, customer-service reps on whether they can keep their customers happy. Theoretically, all these concerns add up to a healthy bottom line. But if people don't really understand the connection and aren't in the habit of seeing (or caring about) the financials, then what happens? They focus on their own goals and don't really give a damn about how the company is doing.

The open-book company's week-in, week-out concern for financial performance can seem like small-minded, bean-counter-mentality number crunching. What's wrong with this place? Nobody values elegance or quality or market share or shipping volume or happy customers any more—all they care about is profits. And this problem needs resolution, because any healthy company needs people who do care about all those intermediate goals.

The keys to the resolution? (1) Create a balanced scorecard for the company or business unit as a whole—a scorecard that includes nonfinancial goals along with financial goals (see Chapter 5). (2) Make sure that departmental scorecards include those intermediate or operational goals (such as shipping volumes or customer-complaint rates) along with financial data. (3) Make sure that people understand the relationship between the goals they value and how the company does. A healthy bottom line does indeed depend on what they do. And their job prospects, ultimately, depend on a healthy bottom line. This is what's known as a win–win situation.

Because open-book management is a system, it can be hard to know where to start. It isn't difficult to implement statistical process control or the manufacturing technique known as single-minute exchange of dies. You appoint or hire a teacher, set aside time for classes, and give people a chance to put what they have learned into practice. But how do you implement open-book management? Setting up a bonus plan won't do it. Neither will teaching people the basics of business. Open-book management is a loop, in which every aspect supports and reinforces the others. It can be puzzling as to where, and how, to break into that loop.

The next several chapters address this problem in detail. It's worth addressing in detail because plenty of companies have blundered when they embarked on the open-book process. One CEO "sat people down for three hours and dumped all the financial statements on them." You can imagine the response. The owner of a small manufacturing company decided to begin by giving employees responsibility for scheduling. Result: disaster. ("When people haven't had any responsibility for scheduling, products just don't get out the door. You realize you have to have some classes on scheduling.") Still another chief executive began with a bonus plan—but since employees had no idea what they were supposed to do to earn the bonus, the plan had no visible effect on how they worked.

Finally, open-book management has no end point. This is another way of saying that open-book management requires sustained effort until it becomes an integral part of a company's method of operation. It's not a project, with a beginning, middle, and end. It's not a reengineering initiative that redesigns this or that process. Rather, it's both a system and a practice. It's a way of running a company, and it's a way of thinking about how people in a business work together. It will affect matters as disparate as hiring and training, strategic planning, even corporate structure. On that last point, look at SRC. It has spun off more than a dozen new business units in the last several years, mostly because its open-book system spawned so many business-literate, entrepreneurially minded managers eager to try their hands at running a company.

Self-Reinforcing Change

Even though open-book management poses unique difficulties, its implementation is in some ways easier than that of nearly any other kind of change.

Most change initiatives, after all, are foisted on skeptical employees by managers. They require a hard sell. Employees balk at having to do things in new ways. They don't see what's in it for them. They hunker down, do no more than they have to, and hope to heaven the whole thing will blow over.

This, of course, is likely to be people's initial reaction to open-book management as well. Still, OBM as a process has several things going for it that other initiatives don't.

People can understand the logic of open-book management. Any other initiative may or may not seem reasonable to employees. Why should we be working in teams? Why is this process being reengineered? Managers can try to explain the changes, but if the logic isn't transparent, people are apt to feel they're being duped.

Open-book management, however complex and unsettling it may be at first, at least has a transparent logic. *The goal is to improve our business performance.*

The question "What's in it for me?" is answered right away. Change initiatives demand a lot. People have to learn new tasks, new ways of doing things. They may be expected to attend classes, listen to speeches, do exercises they think are stupid or embarrassing. What's in it for me? is not only a predictable response, it's an eminently reasonable one—and it rarely gets a good answer. Open-book management answers it from the start. The goal is to improve our business performance. If we reach our goal, some of the wealth we create will be shared with everyone.

Because it's a system, it's self-reinforcing—and it changes people. The systematic nature of open-book management may make it hard to know where to start. But once you do start, all the elements are interconnected, and indeed reinforce one another. There's a reason to learn business—so that you can understand the scorecard. Understand the scorecard, and you can see how you're doing on the bonus. If you want to be more than just a passive observer, you have to learn how to move the numbers in the right direction— which means taking advantage of huddles and the other techniques of empowerment practiced by open-book companies.

Over time, learning all this can have a dramatic effect on the way people think and act. "It's really invigorating to see people get turned on about the financials," says Kim Kenyon, co-owner of Pettit Fine Furniture. "Not only for what it does to the bottom line, but for what it does for them personally. It really begins to open up their horizons as they look at their entire lives. They become people who have a future—a future that's much brighter for them now that they're starting to learn about business."

A little historical perspective may be helpful as you consider implementing open-book management.

A century or so ago, companies didn't run the way they do today. Most enterprises were tiny. They included an owner, other family members, maybe an apprentice or two. Larger companies weren't so different; they were little more than collections of small units run by overseers or foremen. How the work was organized, how the employees were deployed, how much they were paid—all this was up to the boss of the unit. Sometimes these units weren't even composed of direct employees of the company. So-called inside contractors would hire their own people, bring them in to a factory, and contract with the corporation for specific pieces of work. The workshop system of organization was transplanted into a new industrial setting.

Not surprisingly, this method of management didn't work too well in the industrial context. Companies had little control over their employees or over the organization of work, so they were prone to bottlenecks and breakdowns. Pay rates and labor practices, because they were decentralized, varied wildly from one department to another. If Frederick W. Taylor hadn't come along, someone else would have, because the new industrial system needed new methods of management. Taylor centralized control over the organization of work and the deployment of workers. He and his followers created central planning departments and central personnel offices, along with standardized job descriptions and pay rates. This bureaucratization of management was an extended process that played itself out over decades. Eventually, it came to be taken for granted as the only way to organize a business.

Today, we're in a period of change at least as rapid as that of a century ago. New technologies and competitive pressures have radically altered the old industrial system. The same technologies and pressures have forced companies to invent new methods of management.

Open-book management is in some ways the culmination of these new methods. It challenges the fundamental assumptions of the industrial age about how people can and should collaborate in the workplace. Open-book companies don't have employees who are hired only to do a specific job. They have people who are expected to think and act like partners in the business. This assumption stands a hundred years of industrial history on its head.

But if it took decades to change managerial practices the first time around, it will probably take decades this time, too. Open-book companies are pioneers—pioneers on what's likely to be a productive but lengthy journey.

Implementation in a Small Company: The Basics

O n the one hand, it's a little odd to be writing about implementing open-book management in "a" small company, as if all small businesses were alike. Small companies differ enormously from one another, and open-book small companies are as disparate a group as any. They are tiny (a dozen employees or fewer) and relatively big (a few hundred employees). They are old-line, family-owned companies and entrepreneurial upstarts. They are software developers, retailers, job-shop manufacturers, business-service companies, restaurants, health-care organizations, wholesalers. Some are owned and run by their founders. Others are owned by investors and run by professional managers. Many—but by no means all—have employee stock ownership plans. A few are nonprofits.

On the other hand, companies below a certain size do have some characteristics in common, and these characteristics inevitably shape the environment for implementing open-book management. For example:

Someone is in charge. Usually it's the founder or the principal owner. Sometimes it's a hired CEO. Whoever it may be, the person at the top really does run the show. He or she knows what's going on in the organization, shapes its direction, and makes most of the key decisions. Compare that situation with that of a large corporation, in which plant managers or local vice presidents may be several layers removed from the chief executive—and the chief executive hasn't much of a clue about what's actually happening on the shop or office floor.

Business processes are relatively simple. I don't mean that they're technologically simple; small companies these days can be as technologically sophisticated as any large corporation. But the basics of how the company makes money—and how each department contributes to that goal—aren't so obscure. Large corporations have huge staff departments and support organizations that bear only a tangential relationship to the delivery of products or services to customers. People in those units often feel (sometimes rightly) that nothing they do can possibly affect the corporation's business performance. In smaller companies, every individual's connection to the bottom line is easier to explain and to perceive.

Small companies often get by without the tools, techniques, and procedures that large corporations take for granted. I don't want to get myself in trouble here, but facts are facts. Plenty of small businesses don't have a budget or an annual plan. Many have no procedures for strategic planning. Some don't bother with regular financial reports. Their information systems are rudimentary, their human-resources practices (hiring, firing, review, promotion, etc.) are ad hoc, their operational procedures are seat-of-the-pants. MBAs are few and far between.

All these traits can indicate strengths! At their best, small companies react fast, move quickly, get things done, while larger competitors still have their MBA-laden task forces studying the issue and developing a plan. But the same traits can also bespeak weakness. CEOs try to do too much. They let themselves be seduced by business opportunities that don't fit with their capabilities or strategic priorities. They run out of money because they haven't planned for their cash needs. Some don't even know *whether* they're profitable, let alone how profitable.

These characteristic traits of small companies establish some critical parameters for successful implementation of open-book management.

CEOs have to sign on. CEOs have to be fired up about the possibilities and willing to commit some time and energy to the process. They have to be ready to prod and encourage and support all the folks who are working on implementation. They also—no small matter in a lot of closely held businesses—have to be *ready to share* *full financials with employees.* Without the enthusiastic support of the man or woman in charge, open-book management just isn't going to happen.

The open-book system has to be based on the financial performance of the whole company. It isn't enough in a small company to focus on single-store sales or departmental budgets or gross margin on individual jobs, though all those metrics may function as critical numbers for day-in and day-out tracking. What counts in a small company is how the business as a whole is doing. Small companies live close to the economic margin. If they aren't making money, they aren't creating wealth and they can't pay bonuses, no matter how well any individual work group may be performing.

Every small company has to mount a serious self-assessment of its managerial practices and capabilities before it begins open-book management. An open-book system can't work without regular, accurate financials. It can't work if managers don't know how to read and analyze a P&L or a cash-flow statement. It can't work without good information systems, without a strategic planning process, without budgets, without an ability to forecast. All these elements do *not* need to be in place before a company begins open-book management, but they must be developed as part of the open-book process. Opening the books on a seat-of-the-pants operation will ultimately lead nowhere.

Who plans and initiates open-book management and makes sure that one step follows another? Larger companies need a project team, a plan, and a timeline. (If your company is on the big end of small—a hundred or more employees, say—you may want to turn to Chapter 19, which discusses this method.) But small ones can usually just plunge in. The CEO is likely to be personally involved. He or she will want to get someone from finance—generally the CFO or controller—on board.

Beyond that, it's up for grabs. Ad hoc groups of employees can be signed on to work on bonus plans, to help identify critical numbers, to design scoreboards and come up with games. The whole management team can begin learning the skills of huddling and forecasting, then train their departments. The CFO or another manager can begin teaching the basics of finance. Small companies have come up with dozens of techniques to get started and have pursued the implementation process in any number of ways.

Warm-Ups

The first task any company faces is simply to shake up people's thinking a little—to introduce some of the key concepts of open-book management in an interesting, nonthreatening way. The exhibition games described at the end of Chapter 15 are one such method. There are plenty more. Some ideas:

Guess the shipments. Acorn Manufacturing Company, a Mansfield, Massachusetts, company that makes decorative hardware, started with a guess-the-number-of-pieces-shipped contest. The winner of a weekly contest gets $10, the winner of a monthly contest $40. The purpose? "Just to get people more aware of some basic numbers," says vice president Eric DeLong.

Focus on the targets. The lower-level managers at ACuPowder International LLC, in Union, New Jersey, never saw the annual plan when the company was a division of Alcan Aluminium Ltd., so they never knew what targets the organization was shooting for. After a local management group bought the company, president Ed Daver and vice president for finance Michael Kudryk created a game they dubbed Business Baseball to help managers get up to speed.

Simple rules, says Kudryk. "Each month we score a run if we hit or exceed a target. The competition scores if we don't. There'll be 12 innings in the game—one inning a month—and some kind of gala celebration at the end of the season. A one-page newsletter with the stats will go out each month. It's just intended to raise people's awareness and help them understand how to help in creating profits."

A bonus, not a raise. Jim Annis of Bonanza Nut & Bolt told his employees he was launching a bonus plan based on business performance in lieu of annual raises—and absorbed all the gripes and skepticism. At the end of the year's first quarter, he passed out fat bonus checks along with a sheet showing individuals how much more they had earned under the new system than they would have with a conventional raise. "The difference was quite dramatic," he says dryly—and the employees were suddenly receptive to other open-book ideas.

Go bowling. PARCA is a nonprofit agency in Palo Alto, California, that works with people with developmental disabilities. When executive director Judy Hurley decided to start open-book management, she began by walking into a staff meeting one morning and telling everybody they were going bowling. Groans. Complaints. (We don't have *time* for this!) But Hurley persisted. At the alley, she announced that players would take turns bowling—and that individual scores didn't matter. The team goal was to reach 100 in ten frames. Soon even neophytes were having a good time, and the group began figuring out how many points they needed in each remaining frame to reach their common goal. After bowling, Hurley took everybody out to breakfast and introduced them to OBM.

Classes—and a quiz. William Dee Pickens, president of Pool Covers Inc., in Richmond, California, asked his wife, a former schoolteacher, to teach classes in finance. "She got hold of a workbook called *The Yo Yo Company* and broke the lessons up into eight segments. She'd do some hand-drawn graphics each week and pin them up on the board. Our weekly meetings had been one hour, but we tacked on an extra half-hour for the training." When the classes were through, Pool Covers' sales manager designed a ten-question multiple-choice quiz. Everybody took it, including the managers and Pickens himself—and the sales manager passed out awards to the high scorers.

A skit: "Where *does* the money go?" "We did some playacting," reports Peggy Wynne Borgman, cofounder of Preston Wynne Inc., a health spa in Saratoga, California. Wynne wrote the script. Employees played roles. Wynne's partner played the guitar and sang "The Spa Director's Blues." The plot of the play: where the money goes. "We had an imaginary client who came in and spent $100. We showed where all the money went—and how at the end there was virtually nothing left in the pot. We really wanted people to understand that there are not buckets of money being made in this company, that we have costs to cover."

Contest: bring in referrals. Larry Friedman of Reimbursement Services Inc., in Mt. Laurel, New Jersey, reports that his company started out with a quick, two-week game for sales-related employees. The goal: get the most referrals. The prize: $100. "It surprised everyone," says Friedman. "We put up a chart, and people were filling it in as they went along. They were E-mailing one another. It was a lot of fun."

Hand out some industry numbers. The National Auto Dealers Association, explains Lynn Thompson of Thompson Pontiac GMC

Cadillac, sponsors groups composed of 20 dealers from different locations around the United States and prepares lengthy composite financial statements for each group. Thompson got 13 copies of the full composites and sat down with his department coordinators to review them. "We went over it page by page and department by department, new-car sales and used-car sales, service, body shop. We'd compare them all so that people could really get an idea what we were talking about."

Set a collective goal. Andy Powell-Williams, who manages her husband's Vancouver-area dental practice, launched OBM by asking her staff to set a goal for daily dental-hygiene billings. They did—and they also agreed that 10 percent of revenues over the target would be divided up as a bonus. Average daily billings jumped 12 percent in the first month, easily surpassing the goal. One key: a change in the office's after-hours phone message, requesting that cancellations be made only during office hours (so that patients can be promptly rebooked). Soon after, staff members began investigating the costs of supplies and outside services. "People are starting to think about overall profit and how they can affect it," says Powell-Williams.

Plunging In

Warm-ups, of course, are only that; pretty soon you have to start playing the game. The nice thing about launching open-book management in a small company is that you can start out, experiment, push ahead on a variety of fronts, draw the connections between the various steps, and effect a transformation in 6 or 12 months that might take a larger organization three years to accomplish. There aren't a lot of rules or recipes, but there is, fortunately, a good deal of experience. Here's how three different small companies pursued open-book management.

Glavin Security Hardware Specialists. This 18-employee company in Chicago provides commercial locksmithing services and operates two retail outlets. Owner Tom Glavin read an article about OBM, then attended a seminar, along with his wife and operations manager Julie Lotesto, at Springfield ReManufacturing Corporation. Once they made the decision to go open-book, things happened in rapid succession.

Glavin and Lotesto decided the first step would be to make people aware of the company's sales figures. They posted a sales goal for the month and told employees that if they hit the goal, Lotesto would do the Snoopy dance. (They did and she did). The next month—"after we'd gotten everyone interested," says Lotesto—they divided employees into teams to start those imaginary businesses (see Chapter 6). And six months after that Lotesto began teaching people to understand Glavin's financials.

But it wasn't just training. Lotesto also began posting and distributing numbers. Daily sales totals. Weekly financials. "At our Friday morning meetings they see total sales, cost of goods sold, total gross profit. They know what our targets are, our operational expenses, and our total net profit to date." Meanwhile, too, the company established a simple profit-sharing system: a portion of anything over 6 percent profit went into a bonus pool to be paid out quarterly. To maintain interest, Lotesto started a series of games—a 50-cent pool on monthly sales totals, an extra-time-off incentive for perfect punctuality, a free lunch for the sales staff if they met their weekly sales goals.

A few people, says Lotesto, left the company. "Not everyone was willing to work within a structured business system, which is what open-book management is." But the process, she adds, literally changed the culture of the company; the people who were once just employees were learning to think of themselves as businesspeople. "The more we hit our goals, the more everybody got excited. Now, on the last day of the month I have to kick people out of here because they're so anxious to see what the numbers are!"

Crisp Publications. Crisp, headquartered in Menlo Park, California, has about 50 employees. The company publishes self-improvement and business-training books and provides customized training courses for clients such as Sears. A fulfillment center provides order-fulfillment and customer services for the publications division as well as for several other clients.

Crisp is an ESOP company, and founder Michael Crisp "always believed in the concept of open-book management." So when he read *The Great Game of Business* and met up with some other open-book companies, he was ready to take the leap.

Step one for Crisp: design a bonus plan. "We said to ourselves, the only way this is going to work is if we get everybody's buy-in from the beginning," explains Michael Crisp. "So we said,

'Look, we want to build a bonus plan that will give you an immediate reward and will be congruent with our long-term objectives.'" As a company, Crisp wanted to increase its stock value 10 percent a year. "We went back to the employees and said, 'You build a plan that will assure us a minimum of 10 percent stock appreciation, based on our annual appraisal, and there's no doubt that it will be approved.'"

This process took two or three months, and the plan went through a couple of iterations.

> We had to set the sales forecast and challenge unrealistic goals. We had to look at all the plans in the context of the previous year's operating results. We wanted to make it real enough so that everyone could enter this year with a really good chance of beating their numbers.
>
> Next we held some intensive sessions with each of the groups to show them how the bonus system would work. They saw that if we hit all our goals they could add about eight weeks of pay to their salary, whereas before they might have received only an extra week or two of pay around Christmastime. We also assured them that if they hit their numbers, they'd prosper in the long term, because the value of their ESOP stock would increase correspondingly. That really got them pumped!
>
> Once we locked these things in place, we began putting up scorecards. They're posted throughout the building, so everybody knows the targets and the monthly results for each business unit. We've got a thermometer that captures progress toward corporate monthly revenues; the other postings are simplified income statements.

Crisp Publications played some games. If the company beat the previous year's same-month revenues by 5 percent, employees got a burger-and-beer cookout. If it beat the previous year by 15 percent, the cookout was steak and microbrewed beer. Individual units played games of their own, with goals such as improving the error rate in the fulfillment center and capturing customer information more accurately.

Meanwhile, CFO Brent Youngblood launched a series of classes to teach the basics of business. "We said anyone can show up at the classes," recalls Crisp, "but we expect managers to be there. We'd hold the classes during noon hour over a brown-bag lunch, and Brent would bring nice, fresh Mrs. Fields cookies. We tried to hold it to an hour, but we'd invariably run over. Well, we left the door open. People walking by heard us laughing. They saw the cookies. Next thing we knew, the second series of classes was sold out."

Youngblood's classes started out explaining financial terms and statements, then moved on to topics such as break-even analysis of new products, cash flow, and ratios. "Brent gave homework: 'Here's the information, come back next time and tell me what breakeven is.' We'd go around the table; he'd start in one direction one week, the opposite direction the next. If you got the answer wrong, he just moved on to the next person. But everybody learned and everybody laughed. It was nonthreatening, but it really kept you on your toes. You knew you were going to be called on."

The following year, Crisp put a big banner up in its main entryway: "Let the Games Begin in 1996." Says Youngblood, "The year 1995 was kind of like practice. Now we're getting serious."

Chandler Properties. This 15-employee company in San Francisco manages real estate. Owner Carolyn Chandler read the books about open-book management, attended a seminar, talked at length with a consultant—and then made the decision. She gave all the materials, along with seminar notes and an outline she had prepared, to her company's three-person advisory board and all her employees. She showed them a video about open-book management. "I promised them that not only was I going to learn everything I could about this, but that I was also going to put in a profit-sharing plan and make it retroactive to January. I was making a promise to them so as to keep the pressure on *me*."

Chandler realized that there were some steps her company didn't need—basic business education, for example. "Our people can read financial statements pretty well already. They just don't need a whole lot of business-literacy training." So she moved right on to designing a bonus plan.

First she conducted a peer survey to establish salary ranges, then boosted everyone's salary to the top of the range. "We were saying to them, 'We're going to pay you a top salary *and* we're going to share the profits. In return we want you to work on the business.'" The plan she came up with promised to pay 10 percent of the first x dollars in profits and 20 percent of any profits over x into a bonus pool. To encourage growth, she decided that the x target would be ratcheted upward from year to year.

When she announced the plan, it was July—and Chandler handed out retroactive checks for the first two quarters of the year. "I passed out the checks, and we popped four bottles of champagne. Now *that* got people's attention!"

Soon the company began to hold regular meetings. "We have our open-book meetings every other week, at 3:00 P.M. on Thursdays. We'll go over company news, staff changes, everything. Once a month we'll review the financials and do the forecasting. That really forces them to think about how they can increase the numbers. Then I'll add my bit about new business and how that impacts the income statement." Chandler didn't hesitate to assign people responsibility for individual line items. "We're expanding, and we need another floor, so I had allocated $20,000 for furniture. One of my property managers came in and said, 'Carolyn, why would you *ever* budget $20,000 for furniture? We can do much better than that.' I said, 'Karen, that line item is now yours.'"

Chandler Properties lost about three people "who just couldn't stand the change." Most, says Carolyn Chandler, are flourishing in the new system. "They're really starting to think like business-people." She enjoys it, too. "The time that I used to spend solving problems—troubleshooting—has gone almost to zero. They can really see where this company is going, and they're doing what they need to do."

Steve Wilson's rules for starting OBM. Wilson, founder of Mid-States Technical Staffing Services, is a veteran open-book manager whose experiences I recounted in my first book. Today he has gone out on his own and speaks and consults on open-book management. Wilson has compiled a simple sequence of steps that he feels will get companies (and CEOs) on the right track:

- Identify critical numbers
- Post the critical numbers
- Conduct basic financial training (direct costs, gross margin, SG&A)
- Play a game with a critical number
- Set up a reward (bonus) system
- Stop making decisions!

Hard to argue with any of them.

CHAPTER EIGHTEEN

Implementation in a Small Company: The Ten-Step Process

Stand back a ways and you can see that implementing open-book management means changing a whole system. This process can be broken down into a series of steps, and I'll do that in a moment. (I didn't start out to list ten steps. It just worked out that way.) But—as the examples in the last chapter show—every company's process is different. The steps can be taken in different sequences. They can be combined and recombined in a variety of ways. Sometimes you can skip one, as Carolyn Chandler skipped the business-education portion. So don't take what follows as a recipe, take it as a checklist. Ultimately you'll want to be sure everything on the list is covered.

Two other preliminary points. First, unless your company is very small, no one individual can take responsibility for everything on the list. You may not need a formal OBM project team, as larger companies do, but you'll need volunteers. A CFO or controller who's willing to teach some classes. A group willing to do some research on bonuses. The more people you can get involved in the process, the easier it will be when it comes to getting buy-in. Second, small companies often don't have a lot of spare time and resources. It's easy for them to get caught up in the press of business and forget what they set out to do. So start by charting out a timeline for the whole thing and stick to it. If you don't, it won't happen.

Okay, here are the steps.

1. **Self-assessment.** Before you launch open-book management, take stock of your company. How is morale? If you could wave a magic wand and change something, what would it be? If the employees could wave *their* magic wands and change something, what would that be? Overall, how do they feel about the company, about their management, about their jobs?

   You probably won't need a formal survey, only some questions, some discussion, and a willingness to listen. Lynn Thompson of Thompson Pontiac GMC Cadillac tells how he did it: "I just put a flyer together and said, 'What are the three best things about working at Thompson? What are the three worst things? What are the three things you'd change?' I sent that out to everybody at the dealership, then I went over everything one by one." Thompson heard about some personnel issues, which he took up privately with the people involved. He heard about quality-of-the-workplace concerns. "I addressed every single issue." The point of the assessment? Just to make sure you don't stumble on some fallen logs while you're setting out to reshape the forest. If employees feel they're unfairly treated, or they're working with rotten equipment—if they have any of a host of such grievances—your open-book attempts will get nowhere.

   While you're at it, assess the state of your company's infrastructure—its systems and procedures. Do you have an annual plan? A budget? A strategy? Do you see financial reports regularly? Do you understand the numbers (and believe them)? Who else on your management team is familiar with the financials? Open-book management depends on good systems and structures; if you don't have them, you'll have to develop them.

2. **Self-education.** People have to learn about open-book management. It's a pretty strange notion at first. And it does no good for the CEO (or anybody else in the company) to get all excited about these ideas if nobody else understands them. Maybe you've experienced the "wet shaggy dog" phenomenon. Somebody in the company reads a book, hears a speaker, attends a conference and gets all excited about what he or she has learned. For the next several days that person unloads all that excitement on anyone within earshot, just as a wet dog shakes water on everybody in its vicinity. Before long coworkers

start ducking into empty offices to avoid being cornered in the hall.

So don't expect people to take it in all at once. Instead, convey the message to employees in a lot of different ways, over a few weeks' time. Buy sandwiches and have a talk. Hand out books to read, or post articles on the bulletin board. Show a video about open-book management, or bring in a guest speaker. Send people to conferences or to meetings of other open-book companies and ask them to tell others what they learned. Ask someone to track down open-book companies in your industry and do a report for the group.

Not everyone will take easily to this process. But some will, and they'll help to bring along others. Make sure that all this communication is two-way, not one-way. People will have many, many questions and concerns, and a lot of ideas. Listen up.

3. **Warm-ups.** See the previous chapter. Warm-ups can be goal-setting exercises, learning exercises, games of all sorts.

4. **Identifying critical numbers.** This is really the launchpad for a strategic-planning process, if there isn't one already in place. What are this company's goals over the next year or two? We're talking big-picture goals here; they may have to do with earnings targets, sales-growth targets, market share, diversification, or any other major objective. Clarifying a company's goals is mostly a task for owners and senior managers, but it never hurts to get a lot of feedback from the people who will be asked to implement them. From where they sit, do these goals make sense? What has to happen for those goals to be realized? Every big-picture goal should translate into a series of smaller-picture goals: production targets, efficiency objectives, key financial ratios, and so forth. This *cascade of critical numbers* helps people understand what to organize their efforts around. It keeps everyone on the same page.

5. **Scoreboards.** Critical numbers go up on a scoreboard. The financials—simplified, especially at first—go up on a scoreboard. People need to figure out how many scoreboards a company needs. One big one in the hallway? Separate scoreboards for each department? Then they need to plan the format. Should scoreboards be whiteboards? Computer printouts on

the bulletin board in the lunchroom? Messages sent out over E-mail? Or maybe a protected Web page? A thermometer? Finally, each scoreboard needs a scorekeeper—someone who takes responsibility for keeping it up-to-date and who seeks out ideas for improving it.

6. **Games.** Games can be played around almost any short-term objective, but the most effective games are those that focus on critical numbers. Games get people thinking about how they can affect the numbers. The critical step in any game is to ask people to set their own target, then brainstorm how they're going to reach it. Except in very small companies, you're likely to need a person (or a committee) to act as Games Central, keeping a calendar of games, making sure that one department's game isn't somehow working at cross-purposes to another department, ensuring that rewards for winning are comparable (and not out of line with the game itself).

7. **Teaching business.** People have to begin to understand how the business works, which usually means they'll need some kind of instruction in basic financials. Many companies, like Crisp, ask the CFO to teach some classes. Others bring in a trainer or buy a board game and organize a tournament. Still others send people to outside seminars, such as The Accounting Game. A few can get away with passing out workbooks or computerized self-study programs.

   As soon as possible, instruction in the basics has to lead to instruction in the details of *this company's* financials. Not many employees or line managers want to learn accounting or basic finance for the sake of learning accounting or basic finance. They only want to learn the tools they need to understand how their company is doing.

8. **The transparent company.** The more people begin to understand, the more they can understand—and the more information they can use. Simplified financials can be supplemented with more detailed ones, with lines broken out by department, shift, or work team. Monthly financials can be supplemented with more frequent ones, including weekly and even daily flash reports. Creating good, useful financials is the job of an open-book CFO and his or her team.

9. **Empowerment.** Asking people to take responsibility for their unit's performance can start slowly, with suggestion systems, brainstorming meetings, games. Before long, though, it should proceed to a full-blown huddle system, with departments and work groups assuming regular responsibility for the numbers that they then take to the next higher level in the organization.

10. **Compensation.** The last step in an open-book compensation system is the design of a good bonus system—a system pegged to critical numbers, easy to understand and communicate, generous and fair. This in itself is no small matter! But ultimately you'll want to look at other compensation issues as well. Is base pay competitive? What additional benefits can encourage people to view themselves as owners? Open-book companies often have employee stock ownership plans, stock-purchase plans, 401(k) plans funded with company stock, and so forth. Many of these will be too complex or expensive for some small companies—but you may want to keep them on the horizon anyway, for when the business is bigger and better-heeled.

Evolution of the System

One thing open-book management doesn't do is hold still. Rather, it changes over time as companies learn more and adapt it to their business needs. Here are a few snapshots from small companies that have been practicing open-book management for a while.

Better drill-down financials. At Kacey Fine Furniture, in Denver, controller Mark Smith continues to refine the financial information provided to the retailer's five stores and companywide support departments. Daily flash reports show sales and a few other key numbers. Weekly reports provide near-complete financials in simplified form. A store's weeklies, for example, indicate written sales, delivered sales, and returns, along with five summary expense lines (payroll, employee development, selling-related expense, fixed expense, and outside services). All these numbers are shown in relation to the company's plan, with variances highlighted.

Smith also provides every department with an Excel-based electronic workbook that includes companywide numbers, the department's budget, and the detailed numbers that most affect that department's performance. This helps people see their department as a company within a company, in effect, and start thinking of themselves as businesspeople. Kacey's companywide merchandising unit, for example, styles itself the AAA Merchandising Company. AAA has its own monthly income statement. The statement shows budget and actuals for every line item, with "net profit" at the bottom referring to better-than-budget performance. It highlights key items (such as freight costs) and inventory categories (damaged merchandise, merchandise sold but not delivered, etc.) for which the group is responsible, and that affect Kacey's financial performance.

Setting new goals. Commercial Casework had a record year in 1996. "It was the best year ever!" crows president Bill Palmer. "The goal for new contracts coming in was $6.6 million, and we ended up doing about $7.5 million. Our sales goal was also $6.6 million, and we also did $7.5 million there. And the big one, we had our gross-margin goal of 21.5 percent, and we actually did 22.5 percent. Our original goal for the bonus was going to be a pool of $66,000—but with all those increases the actual payout was $113,000. So people were pretty fired up."

In 1997, Palmer sat down with a new group of employee volunteers to review the company's bonus plan. They fixed some minor administrative matters, like what to do about an employee who leaves the company. Then they took up the matter of goals. A few employees wanted to keep the goals where they were. Nope, said Palmer, we can better our performance. Then the group debated new goals. Palmer wanted high ones; the employees were fearful they'd be out of reach. Finally, they reached consensus: $8.1 million in contract awards, $7.8 million in sales, gross margin of 23 percent.

What persuaded people to agree to those goals, says Palmer, was that the company had actually been performing at the targeted sales-and-awards levels during the last half of 1996—and that the gross-margin target could be reached with fewer mistakes and a little more aggressive pricing. Moral: the *how* of goals is as important as the *what*.

Restructuring the company (and OBM). Share Group, the telephone marketing and fund-raising company, had been growing fast enough to make *Inc.* magazine's 1996 list of the 500 fastest-growing privately held companies. Like a lot of fast growers, it outgrew its corporate structure. "We used to be four divisions: fund-raising, customer service, commercial services outbound, and polling," says general manager Sue Meehan. "In late 1996 we decided these divisions didn't seem to make as much sense as creating only two divisions, one focusing on our nonprofit market and the other on the commercial market."

The restructuring entailed some changes in the way the company's open-book structure operates. Instead of one companywide scorecard meeting each month—with remote sites on-line with each other so they could look at the same financials—the company now held two weekly meetings, one for each division, plus a companywide management-team meeting.

Share's bonus plan, meanwhile, was redesigned to focus on the operational goals of each call center. "Last year our bonus program was tied to companywide objectives," says Meehan. "We had had three recent mergers, so we really wanted to focus people on the goals of the entire company. But if one division did well and another poorly—which is pretty much what happened—the folks in the division that was doing well didn't benefit."

This year, bonuses would be determined for each call center and would be pegged to a critical number known as the labor-cost ratio (total labor costs divided by the center's net revenue). Each center's objective: to reduce the ratio of labor costs to net revenue. A one percentage-point improvement in that ratio (compared to plan) generates a bonus pool of 1 percent of net revenue. (Corporate and staff employees at Share have a similar plan, but it's based on reducing overhead as a percentage of gross profit.)

Call-center employees know how to impact the labor-cost ratio, says Meehan: manage their time more efficiently, make more calls per hour, help ensure that lines are fully staffed. "It's a very easy thing for people to figure out and track. The percentage is displayed in our scorecard meetings every week. There's a plan, and the centers project how they'll do, and [the spreadsheet] actually calculates for them what the bonus pool will be if they hit those projections."

More-elaborate business training. Foldcraft Company used to teach its employees the basics of business with a homegrown series of classes in which students created a chocolate-chip-cookie company. Then it started a new training game known as the School Desk Company game. Here's how CFO Doug Westra describes it:

We have two companies working in the room together—Company A and Company B. We say there are three rules in this game: (1) You're in business to make a profit. We're going to measure that by creating an income statement. (2) You need to generate cash. We'll follow that by creating a cash-flow statement. (3) You need to increase the value of your business. That we measure with the balance sheet.

So we set up the two teams, maybe eight to ten people on each. They start off on equal ground. The game lasts for a week, two hours a day on Monday, Wednesday, and Friday. We get them started by saying, "Okay, here are the materials you'll need to buy to make desks." We give them their purchases and how much that's going to cost. We tell them what equipment they'll need to run their business. We tell them how much their monthly operating expenses will be.

We start the game. "Okay, Uncle Albert passes away, and he leaves you $40,000 cash. All your life you've been thinking, 'Gosh, this is a great business . . . if I only had the money I could get into it!' You've done your research, and you know how much it costs to make a unit, what you can sell it for." Then it's January first. The first thing they do is draw their factory. They have a big, long table they sit at, with a big, white piece of paper all the way down the middle of it. Then we tell them that in the first month, they have to make ten desks. So we dump a whole box of Lego pieces there, and they have to produce those desks. In the first month, the same thing happens with each team. We stop at the end of the month and fill out the scorecards. We go through the three statements and teach them how to fill them out.

Once they get their operating expenses on the income statement, they have to pay us. Physically. Operating expenses for the month may be $4,200, but how much of that amount do you actually pay me? They ask things like, "Wait, is there depreciation in that operating expense?" Or, "Oh yeah, we're only supposed to pay you only $4,000 now." They have $44,000 of play money to use, which Albert left them.

Then we go into February. We design the game so that one of the teams decides to invest $500 in a training program. That company spends the additional $500 for the month, and that's the only difference between the two companies. At the close of that month, each team fills out the three statements again. Then we stop, flick on the overhead, and show visually how Company A is doing compared to Company B. There are three critical measures we look at. (1) Who made the most money? Well, in this month, Company B has more money because they didn't spend anything on training. (2) Who has the most cash? (3) Who has increased the value of their business most? After the second month, Company B is ahead.

Then comes March. As we play the game, we set up other rules, such as "Your customer will pay you 30 days after you ship. You have to pay your suppliers on the 15th day following the month you purchased." At certain points, we have to stop and exchange money.

We run the game for six play months. In April, both companies' compressors go down. They both have $1,000 bills they need to spend to repair the equipment. But Company A, which has invested in the teamwork and cross-training, gets up and running quicker! Company B loses a whole day of production! As a result, Company B doesn't ship all the units they're supposed to. We go ahead and fill out the scorecards, pointing out how managerial decisions and unexpected glitches impact the bottom line.

Now, the number one rule in the game is: if you run out of cash, you lose. There are no loans. Then we get into May, and poor Company B . . . It gets the extra seven units it didn't ship last month shipped, but now they're five units behind. What happens? They run into a quality problem. They have scratched desktops. Meanwhile, Company A, through the training investment, was able to implement a quality-first program. So then they get to see the effect poor quality can have on the bottom line.

We get into the next month, June, and Company B has four lost-time accidents, and they try to implement a safety program. But Company B's insurance premium is now much higher than Company A's, since their workers' comp costs went up. What eventually happens is that Company B runs out of cash. Its supplier comes in on the 15th of the month and says, "I want to be paid for last month's purchases." Then, they go to their envelope of cash and they don't have enough. Then the game ends, we pull everyone together, we put up the final statements for each team.

Afterwards, we put out the Foldcraft Company statements, which are measured the same way as in the game. We tell them, "See? It's no different here in our company than it is playing the game." We draw correlations between the game and the company regarding quality, and safety, how money is paid and when. When we let them go, we tell them: "Learning how to keep score is about one-tenth of the issue here. You know now how we keep score, and how the numbers go on the different statements, but now your task is to go back out into your unit and have an impact on that bottom line."

As these examples suggest, a company that is well into open-book management has at least three major tasks. It has to broaden and deepen the practice of open-book management, so that it is an integral part of the corporate culture. It has to adapt the practice to the changing needs of the company. And it has to keep on involving people—more and more people—in open-book management.

Broadening and deepening OBM

Broadening open-book management means spreading it to every nook and cranny of the business. The delivery people. The folks in the warehouse. The information-services department. People in the sales office in Texas. Small companies don't have the problem faced by larger organizations of implementing open-book management in hundreds of facilities involving thousands of people. But plenty of less-than-huge enterprises have several departments, business units, or locations. Don't forget them!

And while we're on the subject of broadening, don't forget new people, either. A lot of small companies—particularly those that are growing fast—add a substantial number of new people every year. They'll need to be introduced to the concept of open-book management. They'll need to learn what a critical number is, and how to take part in a huddle, and how the bonus system works. They'll need the same training in business basics that everybody else got.

Deepening open-book management means changing and refining the practice, so that the tools and techniques are more and more useful. Foldcraft designed a better training program. Kacey Fine Furniture developed more-useful financials. Bonus programs evolve, as do huddles and other mechanisms to engage people in the business. Companies invent more-imaginative games and more-useful scoreboards. One of the striking facts about the evolution of open-book management is that its adherents have formed a kind of community of practice, sharing ideas and experiences with one another through networking groups, conferences, and a newsletter.

As with TQM practitioners a decade ago, they are learning most from one another.

Adapting OBM to the changing needs of the company

Share had to restructure its huddle system and bonus plan as it grew. Commercial Casework (and many other companies) set new goals from year to year. Companies will have new objectives, new critical numbers, new products and services, new opportunities. Open-book management has to evolve so that it is serving the company's objectives, not getting in the way.

It's wise to remember the limitations of open-book management in this context. It is no substitute for any of the other things a company has to do right in order to succeed in business. Companies need a vision of where they're going and a smart strategy for getting there. They need astute deployment of financial (and other) assets. They need to hire and manage their people wisely. They must be able to deliver value to a customer consistently and to innovate in a timely fashion. Open-book management isn't supposed to replace any of these business virtues. Rather, it helps a company pursue its objectives more effectively, by getting everyone working together toward the same ends.

Involving more and more people

When you launch open-book management, you're likely to find people mentally taking sides. A minority—10 to 20 percent—will love the idea and leap in. About the same number will hate it and will bad-mouth it. Most will wait to see what happens. As time goes on, the job is to win over and involve that silent majority.

There's no magic bullet; you just have to do what you say you're going to do, help people learn, make sure they're rewarded fairly for their efforts. If you're successful, people who can't or won't adapt to the new system will leave. You'll never have 100 percent eager, active participation, of course—people aren't like that. But you can have a sizable majority of your employees solidly behind the open-book approach and involving themselves in helping to run the business.

One key to this involvement is to have fun: play games; buy lunch; throw parties. Open-book management is a people-oriented philosophy; it says, in effect, We're all in this together and we'll sink or swim based on our own efforts (and a little luck). Might as well have a good time along the way.

Open-book companies have two goals. They seek to be high-performance organizations, companies that deliver financial performance at or near the top of their industries. They also seek to be great places to work—companies where a job is more than just a job, where people can learn, grow, expand their horizons, build their own security, even make some real money. The path to these objectives is not to assume that open-book management can be installed, implemented, and forgotten about. It's an approach that has to engage and involve the people in a company, so that they can create their own futures.

Implementation in a Large Company: The Basics

Changing a large company is a fundamentally different process from changing a small one, and it's only partly because of the different scale involved.

Granted, scale can't be ignored. A company that makes *Fortune*'s list of the 500 biggest companies—or even a mythical list of the 1,000 or 2,000 biggest—is likely to have dozens or hundreds of facilities and thousands of employees. Introducing new systems and teaching new patterns of thought and behavior on this scale doesn't happen overnight.

But scale isn't the only problem. (If it were, it could be solved simply by starting small and moving outward, one department or facility at a time.) The real problem is that the typical large corporation is a fundamentally different animal from the typical small company. It works differently. It faces different sets of constraints. It has different characteristic strengths and weaknesses. Anybody who proposes to implement open-book management in a large company needs to understand the effects of all these factors—and to plot a course that skirts all the predictable obstacles they present.

Let's take these up one at a time.

Authority (and politics). In small companies, one person is in charge. The CEO knows most of what takes place in the shop or the office. When he or she decides to change things, people pretty much assume that something is going to change. (Whether they *like* the change or not is a different story.)

The CEOs of big companies have a different set of concerns, and those concerns rarely revolve around the shop or office floor.

The top dogs of a large corporation plot big-picture strategies. They decide what to acquire or sell. They figure out where to invest. They think about Wall Street, and their boards of directors, and, sometimes, who will succeed them. I have never seen a case when the CEO of a large corporation personally decided to implement open-book management—or any other new approach to the organization of work and the workplace. CEOs worry about *what* will get done. Not many of them worry about *how* it gets done.

But if it isn't the CEO who's making the decision to implement open-book management, who is it? Typically, it's a regional chief, or the head of a subsidiary, maybe an operations VP or even a plant manager. But if you're embarking on a project as bold as open-book management and you don't run the company, you have to be pretty well situated. You have to be confident that the chief (or the chief's top deputies) will support you. You have to be able to ignore or ward off the skeptics and naysayers elsewhere in the corporation—because you can be sure they'll be watching for signs that you're screwing up. Managers in a large corporation work in a Darwinian world, where people either win or lose. If you lose, somebody else wins.

Moral: it can take a remarkable individual—or a team of individuals, working together—to sponsor and support a venture as dramatic and thoroughgoing as open-book management in a big corporation. It's always safer to do what you're supposed to do, to take only modest risks, to avoid rocking the boat.

Constraints. Big companies also face different sets of constraints, both internal and external, from those faced by small companies.

On the outside, they're more likely to be publicly traded, and hence subject to the scrutiny of both Wall Street and the press. They're more likely to be unionized (or to face the threat of a union-organizing campaign). They're more likely to hold government contracts or to be major employers in an area, and hence to show up on the radar screens of politicians and regulatory agencies. They have a legal department whose job is to watch out for possible lawsuits. All these constraints obstruct a large company's freedom of action—if not directly, then indirectly, by making managers cautious.

On the inside, the constraints can be even more powerful. Big companies are governed by bureaucratic rules and procedures. Those rules and procedures can't all be abolished—after all, you want people in one location to work under the same regimen as their

colleagues in other locations, and you want everyone to be working on a coordinated strategy. But what happens when you want
to change things? Rules and procedures have to be rewritten or
else circumvented. The people responsible for implementing those
rules and procedures—a small army of bureaucrats and middle
managers in many corporations—get scared and angry. The employees affected by the change hear mixed messages. Some take
the opportunity to complain (loudly) about how management doesn't
know what it's doing.

These days, as I've said more than once in this book, the problem of change is even worse, just because so many corporations
have launched so many ill-fated change initiatives that even the most
enthusiastic employees have to be a little jaded. Small companies,
for all their limitations, at least allow day-in, day-out, face-to-face
communication between the people in charge and those on the
shop floor. The latter group can usually make a pretty good assessment of how seriously to take the boss's (or the plant manager's) latest kick. Big companies, large and impersonal, don't allow that kind
of human judgment. People's natural reaction: We'll wait and see.

Characteristic strengths and weaknesses. Small companies often
suffer from a dearth of resources, from lack of expertise, from in-
adequate systems and procedures. Big companies don't. They have
plenty of money available. They have or can hire people who are
experts in just about any field. They have well-developed systems
and procedures. You want a videoconference set up? No problem—
just call the communications folks, get your assistant to take care
of the paperwork, and you'll have your videoconference (in the
special videoconference room). The average small company would
no more do a videoconference than hold a retreat on the moon.

All those systems and resources, of course, have their downsides
(as many, many big companies have discovered in the last decade
or so). Large corporations waste money. They throw dollars at
problems and figure that'll solve them. They get so tied up in systems
and procedures that they are outmaneuvered by smaller, nimbler
competitors. When they implement a change initiative, the typical
drill is to get the budget approved, hire the consultants, set up the
training classes, issue the manuals—and expect things to change
right now. Should we be surprised when nothing happens? Then,
too, the normal operation of large companies often militates against
change, or at least against planned-and-organized change. People

who begin to change a department or business unit suddenly get transferred. Whole segments of the company are reorganized and recombined.

Taking all these factors into account, it may seem a miracle that big companies ever manage to reshape themselves effectively. Certainly it isn't astonishing that a transformation as far-reaching as open-book management should have been pioneered by small and midsize companies. And yet, a handful of big companies *have* found effective ways to launch the open-book process. They recognize the obstacles and don't expect everything to change all at once. But they also recognize the opportunity to make a change that their competitors will find hard to emulate—a change that alters the way people throughout the organization think of their work and their workplace. This chapter lays out the steps involved in getting started. The next one tells the story of a corporation that has been implementing open-book management for the last few years.

Get Ready, Get Set

So let's say that someone—a regional VP, the head of a subsidiary, someone with enough authority and personal clout to pull it off—has decided to implement open-book management in at least one business unit of a large corporation. What happens next? Unlike in a small company, you can't just pass out a few books, watch a video, and plunge in. So the first job is to pick an implementation team—a group of people, preferably volunteers, who will take responsibility for designing and launching the open-book system. The team needs to include a senior manager or two. It should involve people from a variety of departments and organizational levels. It ought to have someone from finance, preferably the chief financial officer or controller. Mostly, though, it needs a leader, a champion—*someone whose job it is to make open-book management happen.*

The champion

Identifying and appointing a champion can be the biggest challenge any large corporation faces. The champion can't be a senior manager who is already putting in 60-hour weeks before adding open-book to his or her other responsibilities. Nor can it be an assistant or newcomer without the knowledge or authority to make things happen. Don Robb, the Donnelley employee whose story is told in the next chapter, was an ambitious manager who had done stints in sales and organizational development when he was given the assignment of implementing open-book. Champions at other companies have been internal consultants, veteran (and well-respected) middle managers, HR directors, even controllers. Wherever they come from, implementing open-book management has to be one of their key responsibilities, and the success of open-book management must be a key measure by which their performance will be judged.

This is not a job for just anybody! Champions need the ability to learn and communicate new ideas. They have to be patient, persuasive, imaginative, creative. They'll need to win the respect of frontline employees, figure out ways to get supervisors and middle managers on board, cultivate support from senior managers. Finding such a person can be a chore, but it shouldn't be impossible. Even in these post-reengineering days, most large corporations have a deep reservoir of talented people looking for new challenges. And companies that have already embarked on the process discover that open-book management is a challenge that gets people's blood flowing. It's a chance to do something that will make a difference.

Self-education

Once constituted, the team has to learn about open-book management. They have to do their homework. Where to start? Most companies begin with books, articles, and videos. If everyone doesn't have time to read, some members can be appointed readers and report back to the rest of the group. Eventually, some team members can attend seminars or conferences on open-book management, while others take on the task of calling up or visiting other open-book companies.

This self-education process is critically important, and not only so that team members will know what they're doing. As soon as word gets out that the company is embarking on open-book management, everyone else will start asking questions. People will want to know what this is all about, does it really work, what's this we hear about a new bonus system, how does this fit with the TQM stuff we did last year, and is it true that we're going to have to go to accounting class? The implementation-team members may not know all the answers right away. But the better they're equipped to deal with the questions, the easier the whole thing will be.

Self-assessment

The next step: take stock. Find out what's going on in the company before you start to change it. The reasons for this step aren't hard to fathom. Some companies have a variety of hidden problems—personnel issues, systems and procedures that don't work (and everyone except the bosses *knows* they don't work), misconceptions and misunderstandings about where the company is headed, and so on. Any of these problems can be a major obstacle to the implementation of open-book management. If the people responsible for implementing it don't know about them, the whole thing will fail—and no one will quite know why.

How to do it? Donnelley used focus groups. A more common approach is to survey the workforce. Boundless Technologies, for example, asked questions about how well employees understood the business's strategy and financial performance, then wound up its three-page questionnaire with five open-ended queries:

- What can the company do to make you more productive?

- What should the company do to become more profitable?

- What's the biggest problem the company needs to remedy?

- What can the company do to make your job more satisfying?

- What's the biggest opportunity for improvement the company should pursue?

To ensure confidentiality, Boundless allowed people to leave their names and departments off the survey and asked an outside organization to tally the results. "The most important part is looking through the responses to those open-ended questions," said Steven Green, the company's director of human resources. "We've gotten a lot of good information from the people who are doing the job every day."

The Great Game of Business—a spin-off of Springfield Re-Manufacturing Corporation that teaches SRC's open-book system—sells a booklet containing sample questionnaires for both employees and managers. A survey or appraisal process, says the booklet, "is the first step in involving people in the business."

Planning implementation

While conducting the appraisal, the implementation team needs to map out a strategy and timeline. How will open-book management be introduced to the company's managers? To its nonmanagement employees? Will there be pilot projects, and if so, in which units? Once the pilot projects are completed, how and where will the open-book process be rolled out? Which steps will come first, and which ones later?

These questions don't allow for easy answers, because every company is different. Companies with many similar locations (stores, distribution facilities, etc.) face one set of challenges and opportunities, while companies with large, integrated facilities (big offices or manufacturing plants) face another set. The implementation scenarios that follow suggest some possibilities, but any generic plan will have to be adapted to an individual company's needs and situation.

Every open-book team will have one task in common, however: involving other people. That may be the single most important key to success.

After all, what happens when you try to change any organization of human beings? People get excited—and nervous. They gossip. If they aren't included in the process, they feel left out. Those in authority worry that they're going to lose their power. People who feel they always get the short end of the stick figure they're going to get it yet again.

The antidote to these perfectly predictable reactions is simple. Get people involved. Set up task forces, subteams, work groups. Designate open-book champions for every department or shift and charge those people with spreading the word. Line up a "sponsor team" of senior managers to ensure resources and support.

Above all, communicate. Put out a newsletter that explains what open-book management is and what's being discussed. Hold informal brown-bag lunches to answer questions. Make the books, articles, and videos used by the implementation team available to everybody for borrowing. (The folks at GT Development, in Seattle, wrote a one-act play to explain some aspects of the company's new open-book system.) Do all this even before you start the implementation process, and you'll find it will go a whole lot smoother than any change initiative before or since.

Steps To Implementation

Even small companies rarely start everything involved in open-book management all at once. It's just too time-consuming. You can't teach the business, figure out your critical numbers, redesign your compensation system, and so forth at the same time. In larger companies, a stepwise sequence is even more important—which raises the question of where to begin.

Maybe we should start somewhere else—where *not* to begin.

I don't recommend beginning with business education, for example. Unless people understand the importance of what they're studying—unless they understand *why* they're expected to learn all those numbers and terms—most will be at a loss. Their eyes will glaze over. It won't sink in. Nor do I recommend starting with revamping the bonus system. An open-book bonus has to be tied to a scoreboard, and people have to understand the scoreboard. Until they do, the bonus will be as meaningless as most bonuses in conventional companies.

Instead of starting with any single step, I suggest a two-pronged approach. One team begins creating open-book *experiences* on a small scale. Another team designs an open-book *system* that can operate across the entire company or business unit.

Open-book experiences

What's involved in open-book management? When you boil it down, all it means is learning to understand and track some key numbers, learning how to affect those numbers, and sharing in the success when the numbers move in the right direction. This is a pretty easy experience to capture on a small scale.

One fruitful approach is to launch a game. Gather the members of a department together. Talk with them about the numbers that measure the effectiveness of their work. Ask them to set a goal for the next month or quarter and to design a scoreboard to track their progress. Together, figure out an appropriate reward for hitting the goal. (Maybe the company buys lunch.)

This is the simplest way to get started on open-book management, and it's one of the most effective. At Columbia Regional Medical Center Southwest Florida, a unit of Columbia/HCA, chief operating officer Pat Ekdahl established her pilot bonus plan—essentially a game—for the center's 200-plus operating-room personnel (see Chapter 15). Other large companies have set up even more ambitious pilot projects.

A division of a large telecommunications company, for instance, decided in 1996 to experiment with open-book management. The division's internal-consulting unit got the job of coming up with a plan and then implementing it. A five-person team was assembled, and team members began their self-education process. They decided to work, at first, with the units within the division that handle information systems, security, facilities management, and so forth for the company's big sales-and-service centers.

Support organizations such as these units don't have income statements and balance sheets. What they do have is budgets, which is what the consulting team focused on. In most support units, they figured, employees never see the budget and so don't give a second thought to, say, booking last-minute flights or sending packages by overnight rather than second-day delivery. Managers think they have better things to do than watch every dollar—and if they overspend, well, all the more reason they should get a bigger budget next year. Money trickles away.

In an open-book company, the team figured, everyone in a department would both watch and take responsibility for their budget—and would be rewarded not for spending money but for saving it. The plan they came up with was designed to implement this idea.

The first step: a daylong seminar run by the team, teaching the basics of open-book management and the specifics of the company's budget processes. Participants learned what expense-tracking and variance reports were. They did exercises illustrating the financial impact of everyday decisions. A professional-quality manual written and produced by the team served as both textbook and handy reference guide once the seminar was over.

But the seminar wasn't merely classroom learning, it was also the launchpad for a new open-book process, which the participants then were charged with implementing. In the new process, all employees in a department take part in setting their group's business objectives (within the framework established by senior management) and determining the budget they need to support those objectives. Then they forecast, track, and monitor their spending each month. The consulting team created an electronic tracking tool that employees can retrieve from a company Web site and use much like a checkbook, entering expenses as they are incurred. At the end of the month, the tool provides instant totals for every line item. At the same time, a newly established budget-review group—the managers of each department plus two elected staff representatives—reviews every department's expenditures and approves the next month's budget requests. If the organization comes in under budget while achieving its objectives, everyone gets an agreed-upon incentive award, such as a gift certificate or an extra day off.

Syncor International Corporation took a similar approach. A leading distributor of time-critical radioactive pharmaceuticals, the company has roughly 120 facilities (known as pharmacies) across the United States, which serve hospitals and other medical providers. An open-book team led by human-resources director Joyce Douglas designed a four-month pilot program, which it implemented in five facilities. The facilities were among Syncor's larger ones—averaging 25 employees apiece—but weren't distinctive in any other way; that is, they weren't exceptionally successful or exceptionally unsuccessful.

The team created a training program, with teaching materials, which explained each facility's financials. They mapped out a series of meetings in which a pharmacy's employees would learn where the money went and would brainstorm ways of controlling expenses. They set up a short-term bonus program: one-third of all money saved would go into a bonus pool to be divided equally among employees.

At the end of four months, the team judged the results successful. Four of the five facilities saved a total of roughly $100,000. Financial performance was better—and turnover lower—in the experimental open-book facilities than in similar non-open-book facilities. In 1997, the company decided to roll out the program to at least 30 more pharmacies.

Designing the system

Games and pilot projects don't mean anything, of course, unless they lead to something else. So implementation-team members soon have to set to work designing the rest of the company's open-book system. There are five steps.

1. Identifying critical numbers. This shouldn't be as hard in a big company as in a small one, because somebody, somewhere, is likely to know what those numbers are. The company has strategic objectives and financial goals for its business units. The accounting department should be able to provide plenty of data linking the work (and the budgets) of individual departments to business-unit performance. Line managers will almost certainly have rule-of-thumb numbers that they watch carefully, because they know they'll be judged on whether they make those numbers. The critical-number team's job is to gather up this data, link it, make the connections understandable—to create that cascade of critical numbers that is central to any open-book system.

2. Creating scoreboards. Getting the word out in a big company can be hard. If most people use computers—and if the company has a good E-mail system or even an intranet—then electronic scoreboarding is a logical choice. Otherwise people have to build scoreboards for all the lunchrooms, break rooms, and work areas necessary to make sure they're seen by every last employee. The team also has to figure out what to do about remote employees— salespeople, service technicians, traveling executives, and any other people whose work regularly takes them off-site. E-mail again may be a possibility. One trucking company uses voice mail for this purpose; the CEO broadcasts a weekly report on critical-number performance to every driver's mailbox, and the drivers hear it when they call in to check their messages.

3. Planning the business-literacy training program. A unit of Intel Corporation bought a business-simulation board game and organized a tournament; teams of employees played for prizes. Wascana Energy developed a computer-based business-simulation game and did the same thing. Wabash National pays a local professor to come in and teach business and rewards employees who take the course with a wage incentive. There are a hundred different ways to get people involved in learning the basics of business. But the team will have to plan the program, do up the budget (and get it okayed), buy the products, and line up the trainers. Most big companies will have training departments that can help with this, and someone from HR should almost certainly be involved on this team.

4. Building structures for empowerment. One step for this team is to brainstorm small ways in which people can begin to affect their work areas: suggestion systems, investment-justification forms, and the other tools mentioned in Chapter 8 are all possibilities. But its real job is to design a full-blown huddle system.

This is one area where the rubber will meet the road, because a true huddle system will involve every manager in the company, right up to the person in charge. If people are serious about open-book management, they'll learn what's involved in huddling (Chapter 9) and make a commitment to do it regularly. The project team will need the active, explicit backing of senior management, because every other manager's first reaction will be, "Oh, no, not another meeting—and every week? You've gotta be kidding!"

5. Designing an open-book bonus plan. One group of team members will have to explore options and propose a plan to senior management. This is the other area where the rubber meets the road, because when you get into compensation you're entering a rat's nest of possible problems. It isn't just that anything involving compensation is loaded, though that's certainly the case. It's that the whole idea of an open-book bonus system can run afoul of any number of assumptions, practices, and regulations. Among them are the following:

- In most corporations, people expect annual raises—and hope for a bonus on top of that. In an open-book company, the bonus (and every other ownership-building tool, such as an employee stock ownership plan) is an integral part of the compensation system. It may take the place of annual increases.

- Most large corporations have companywide compensation policies. If open-book management is being implemented in only one division or business unit, you're effectively asking the company to make an exception to its policies. This can take some doing.

- Labor law rears its ugly head. According to federal law, no labor-management committee appointed by management can negotiate binding compensation plans. You don't run into this problem if you don't include any nonexempt employees; if you do, check with a labor lawyer to be sure you're not getting into trouble.

- An open-book bonus plan typically includes everybody—which may mean altering the bonuses paid to executives, salespeople, and other favored groups. They'll howl.

Can all these problems be circumvented? Yes. Companies have done it. Be sure to include at least one compensation specialist on this committee, along with the highest-ranking manager you can get. Consult with experts and other open-book companies as necessary. It's worth it. A true open-book compensation plan is the key to the whole system. In the final analysis it's what enables employees to view themselves as businesspeople without feeling that they're being taken for a ride.

Putting all these steps together, of course, is a challenge for any company. But it can be done! The story of RR Donnelley & Sons—which may be the biggest company yet to implement open-book management in a thoroughgoing way—shows how.

Implementation in a Large Company: The Donnelley Experience

RR Donnelley & Sons Company, with 38,000 employees, is the nation's largest commercial printer.* The company's home is in Chicago, but this story is about the Northeastern Division, which includes two big plants in Lancaster, Pennsylvania. The division, run by senior vice president John Hallgren, serves some of Donnelley's biggest customers. The 1,200-employee East Plant churns out millions of copies of *TV Guide*, *Reader's Digest*, and the *New York Times Magazine*. The 1,000-employee West Plant, a few miles away, produces catalogs and telephone directories for customers such as Williams-Sonoma and Bell Atlantic.

In the mid-1990s, the division, like much of the rest of the company, found itself in a curious position. On the one hand, business was good. The company had recently landed a couple of big contracts, and the East Plant was being expanded to accommodate them. "We were in a growth mode," remembers one manager. "We didn't have profitability problems. Some people said we had no compelling need to change."

On the other hand, a lot of managers felt maybe the company would do well to change now, while things were positive, rather than wait for them to get worse. The printing industry, after all, was experiencing all the furious pressures that were shaking up businesses all over the United States. Fast-changing technologies. More—and fiercer—competition. A different marketplace. Donnelley's business no longer looked the way it had in the past.

---

* Portions of this chapter (in different form) appeared in "Opening the Books," *Harvard Business Review*, March–April 1997.

Once, for example, it could sign a contract with Western Electric to produce Yellow Pages directories for telephone companies all over the country and be assured of comfortable margins on the deal. Now Donnelly had to court many more customers—and every one wanted the cheapest possible price. Worse, there were now several competitors with nearly as much high-quality capacity as Donnelley.

Donnelley's senior managers hadn't exactly been sitting still in the face of all these changes. They were investing in new equipment and in whole new businesses. They were pursuing big contracts aggressively. On the shop floor, they were sponsoring many of the same workplace initiatives instituted in other companies. Quality circles. A "Do It Right the First Time" quality program. Single-minute-exchange-of-dies (SMED) training. Donnelley called these initiatives high employee involvement, or HEI. HEI programs, in theory, taught press crews and other frontline employees the skills they needed to work more effectively.

All this activity had beneficial effects, which was why the company was doing well. But it was hard for managers—particularly operational managers—to get too complacent. The HEI programs, for example, were fraught with contradictions. People learned new skills, but didn't always use them. They were given new responsibilities on the job, but often lacked the information they needed to carry out those responsibilities. "We were asking employees to become higher performers, to make decisions that supervisors used to make," says John Bernard, who runs the West Plant's directory module. "But we weren't giving them the tools they needed, like how much does a pound of paper cost, how much does a plate cost?" After a few years, indeed, all the HEI programs seemed to fade into a kind of corporate haze. People in the Northeastern Division knew there was this thing called HEI. But most would have been hard-pressed to say exactly what it was or what difference it really made.

Donnelley needed a new idea—and when John Hallgren heard Jack Stack of Springfield ReManufacturing Corporation speak at a conference, he figured he might have found one. Hallgren took first one group of managers and then another out to SRC to see the company's Great Game of Business open-book system in action.

They were impressed. Open-book management, they realized, wasn't just HEI in another guise. For one thing, it was a systematic, thoroughgoing approach to reshaping the business, not an initiative that would be implemented and then forgotten. For another, it focused on real business objectives, not just on this or that operational goal. Open-book management wasn't so much the solution to a particular problem as it was, in one manager's words, "a way of getting 1,100 people in one facility focused on the health of the business so that we could sustain the growth we were experiencing."

Hallgren and his lieutenants decided to implement it. In early 1995, they appointed a manager named Don Robb to spearhead the effort. By early 1997, they were well into it, though by no means finished with the implementation. Here, step-by-step, is how Robb and Donnelley did it—and where they were as this book went to press.

Getting Buy-In

With conventional initiatives, a company's decision to hire consultants is usually the critical step. The consultants hand out the reading materials, teach the classes, and work with managers and employees to implement the prescribed changes. Robb hired some consultants affiliated with SRC, but figured they could only help guide the process. A transformation of the magnitude he and his superiors wanted to see would ultimately affect every part of the business. It would require ongoing support and involvement from senior managers, middle managers, supervisors, and frontline employees. No consultant could rally that support; it would have to emerge from the process.

So Robb moved first to involve people. He struck up conversations about open-book management all over the plant. He handed out reading materials. He invited a sizable group of managers and supervisors to an SRC seminar. He arranged for them to stay an extra day. That day, he asked for, and got, a personal commitment to open-book management from each of them. On return, he set up a sponsor team of senior managers to assure resources and support and a project team of managers and supervisors to plan the implementation.

In August 1995, Donnelley kicked off open-book management with a splashy two-day workshop attended by more than 100 managers and supervisors. Jack Stack of SRC gave the keynote speech. The group broke up to discuss the ideas and to talk about ways of implementing them. In the weeks ahead, some 50 people would agree to serve on teams charged with specific tasks.

In effect, the work of these teams *was* the implementation of open-book management at the Northeastern Division of Donnelley. The consultants—a group called Great Game Solutions, from

Calgary, Alberta, headed by David Lough—provided guidelines and advice. Don Robb prodded, encouraged, and counseled his volunteers and set out the framework within which they would work. But it was the teams themselves that created Donnelley's new system.

Assessment

The team charged with assessment, for example, considered and rejected the idea of a written poll, fearing that it would be hard to make sense out of simple responses to a questionnaire. Instead, they decided on an ambitious program of focus groups. "We felt it was much better for us to sit down in small groups, no more than eight or so, and go through a structured conversation in which management was not allowed to participate," explains Herschel Irvin, a manufacturing supervisor who was a member of the team. "It would be a conversation where we did not try to explain, excuse, or stifle any thoughts, but just let people tell us eye to eye what they were thinking."

Each focus group included a manager or supervisor from the area, a facilitator from Donnelley's human-resources department, and six or eight employees representing different levels of experience and skill. The process began in the East Plant, which was to be the first location for open-book management, and later moved over to the West Plant. All told, the team ran some 17 focus groups involving more than 100 employees. Sessions lasted four hours and took place over a three-week period.

In each group, facilitators explained the basics of open-book management and the business rationale for implementing them. Then they asked participants to respond in two ways. First, they were to rate the workplace environment on a variety of measures ("Agree or disagree: People see how they fit into the big picture and how they make a difference."). Second, they could just talk. That, says human-resources coordinator Diane Shaffer, was important in itself. "People have turned in surveys before. They don't know where the surveys go, and they don't see any action as a result. This was a more personal interaction—they saw that listening was occurring. We were recording what they said, writing it up on the board, and they had the opportunity to say, 'No, that's not what I meant.' I think that led them to feel this might really be a first step toward being heard."

Some of what the facilitators heard wasn't so encouraging. Employees feared that open-book would be just another flavor-of-the-month initiative. They didn't understand the financial information they were already seeing and didn't see how more of it would help them. A few felt that managers and supervisors were making exorbitant amounts of money and that trust between managers and employees was at an all-time low.

Still, people were generally hopeful about Donnelley's future and generally positive about their own jobs. When it came to open-book management, moreover, they were remarkably positive. "The final category was really more of a question," says Robb. It was, 'Should we move forward with open-book management?' And overwhelmingly, people said, 'Yeah, we've got to do this.'"

Business-Literacy Training

The team charged with figuring out how to teach business basics was originally one group, but it soon split into two. One took on the task of *developing* a training program, along with whatever materials might be included. The other was charged with *delivering* the program once it was developed.

Development

Right away, the development team homed in on computer-based learning. Classroom instruction seemed too dull and, anyway, would require more classroom space and teachers than would readily be available. A separate program was under way to teach employees computer skills. Some pressroom workers were already using a computerized press simulator to hone their operating skills, and the team had noticed how popular it was. "When we put the simulator in, people were a little reluctant at first," says Wayne Reno, a manufacturing supervisor in the offset-press room. "But when they started getting in there and playing with it, pretty soon we had to put up a schedule! It was fun, but they were learning at the same time. We felt if we could stimulate that kind of enthusiasm, we'd be on to something."

The team brainstormed with consultant Lough, who had developed computer-based business-simulation games for other companies. Says Reno: "We knew we wanted to model it on our business. We knew we wanted things like an income statement, cash statement, a balance sheet, and we wanted them to look like our financials.

We wanted the game to mimic key aspects of our business, but not to be exactly like it. We didn't want people discussing why this particular aspect of the game wasn't exactly like what they actually did."

The result: a fanciful business-simulation game known as Celestial Cheese, which, when you analyze it, looks remarkably like a high-volume printing business. Participants run a company that produces different kinds of cheese on the moon. Explains Reno:

> There are minerals on the moon that are used to make flavors; they're like our inks.
>
> There's Recipe Services, where you design the flavors; that mimics our preliminary department. There's a screen-making process that mimics platemaking or cylinder making. And the actual cheese making mimics the press itself.
>
> You have yearly play and quarterly play. You do your strategizing by year: your capital that you want to invest, how much you're going to put in for training and engineering and safety; what markets you want to go in, where you'll go after your long-term contracts. You have a lot of time during this part of the game play to digest economic information that you have access to, look at trends, look at what your competitors are doing.
>
> After you set your yearly stage, you then enter quarterly play, where you actually have to get the orders, produce the work. If you exceed your capacity that you planned for, you have to farm out, which is very expensive. It's sort of rapid fire. Quarterly play is a timed game; you're actually under time pressure. At the end of that year you're back to annual strategy again.
>
> Our bottom line here is economic value added, EVA. The way you win this game is you drive the stock price up, and the way you drive the stock price up is by increasing your EVA over time. So after the ten years of playing the game, you project out ten years into the future. If you have an EVA that's up and down and up and down, you may end up with a flat projection, whereas if you show an increase in EVA over time, then your stock-price projection is going to be higher.
>
> The game also has a built-in scoreboard. As you're playing the game, the bottom 20 percent of the screen shows you some of the key economic measures, like stock price, EVA, value-added revenue, percent of long-term contracts, and performance

measures. So every move you make you see the effect immediately. You see your stock price change, the EVA change. And
we have warning lights. Red and green lights indicate whether
you may be short on capacity in cheese making, finishing, all
of the other things. There are also measures of customer satisfaction and reputation in your three markets. It doesn't tell
you exactly why you have a problem, but it does say, "Okay, on
Venus, your reputation is suffering, you better go do something about it." It reflects things like your investment in sales,
and whether you've called on these customers.

There's also workplace effectiveness; you have a choice of
working people four, five, six, or seven days a week. You can
invest money in training, you can cut back on training, you
can cut back on wage increases, you can give them bigger increases, you can boost the gain sharing. All of these work to
calculate something called workplace effectiveness, which becomes a limiter on how well the machines perform. Essentially,
if you have a happy workforce, you're going to get more production out of your machines. You can even invest in open-
book management, too!

Celestial Cheese is a complex and sophisticated game. To help
people get up to speed on the computer, the team also helped develop
a computerized version of SRC's *Yo Yo Company* workbook, which
lets people create a highly simplified manufacturing company with
highly simplified financials.

Delivery

The business-literacy-training delivery team, as pressman Tom
Bashore explains it, had five objectives: identify the different groups
of employees that would need training, plan the best strategy for
each group, roll out the programs, support the programs, and get
feedback from the groups. The groups included the management
team, the supervisors, the early adopters, the staff, and the hourly
employees. Managers and supervisors were used as guinea pigs,
playing early versions of Celestial Cheese and helping to find bugs.
The early adopters were critical to the team's strategy; they were
computer-literate people, opinion leaders among the staff and employees, who could be counted on to play the game and informally
introduce it to the others. The idea was to start people off on The
Yo Yo Company, then move on to Celestial Cheese.

But the team was just beginning to wrestle with some interesting and difficult questions. Would employees unfamiliar with computers be willing to learn a complex computer game? Would there be enough computers so that people could play the game regularly? What about the time employees spent playing—was that company time or individual time? And if it was company time, would familiarity with Celestial Cheese ultimately become a condition for continued employment at Donnelley? These questions would be answered over time.

Small Games

Small games, in Donnelley parlance, are short-term, department-based initiatives, with goals set by a group and modest rewards for reaching the goals. The gravure pressroom played a game to boost press efficiency (a measure of throughput that incorporates quality) by 3 percent, then by 3.5 percent, over the previous year's level. The preliminary center played one game aimed at reducing the cost of direct productive materials from $0.11 of every sales dollar to $0.09, and another game aimed at boosting sales revenue per hour worked. Games typically lasted for a couple of months. If they were successful, they might pay out $70 or $75 per person.

Starting these games was one of the fastest and most successful of Donnelley's open-book efforts, mostly because the company's small-games team learned several useful lessons early on.

- *You can start playing games without waiting for the rest of open-book management to cut in.* "We got started right out of the gate," says Edward (Buddy) Ganse, leader of the team. "There was no OBM fanfare. We'd just have some surprise meetings. We'd put teasers up. Then when we started a game, we'd have some kind of commencement—a little fanfare, and a lot of fun. But just for the department that was playing."

- *The primary objective of a game is to teach something about the business.* Don Robb says, "This is all about education." Game players learn the importance of critical numbers. They learn how what they do affects those numbers. The time involved in creating a game may add up—"but if the cost to create the game and the payout is ten grand, that's a good investment in both process improvement and cheap business training for a department. And it's real, job-related business training."

- *A game's target should be measured in dollars.* That, says Ganse, is what differentiated open-book games from various other HEI-related improvement projects, which often didn't engage people's interest. "Money is the universal language. If you put money up there—if money is what you're measuring, tracking, and sharing—you definitely get an additional contribution."

- *A big company needs some kind of representative body to oversee and encourage the games.* At Donnelley, that was the Small Games Council. "We had representatives from all the operational units, and they became the empowering authority for any game," explains manufacturing vice president Geoff Benes. "So if somebody wanted to play a game, they went to the council and said, 'Here's what we'd like to do, here's how we're going to measure it, and here's what the reward system is going to be.'" The council's primary job was coordination—ensuring that games held an educational component, that any payout would be self-funding, and that the scale of effort and reward was commensurate with what other departments were doing. Its secondary job: spread the word; promote game playing. "We wanted to make sure that everybody knew what everybody else was doing," says Benes. "Not to keep people back, but to pull them forward—to make sure that everybody was moving."

For all the successes, Donnelley's small-games group also wrestled with some thorny issues. "Games are the most visible part of OBM—and also the most controversial part," says Don Robb.

One problem was that some staff departments found it hard to come up with games. "We've tried to identify things we could do as games," says Carol Jannello, a customer-service representative. "And it's hard because of the nature of our work. Most of the goals we identify are already within the scope of our job requirements. Some are beyond our control. One thing we discussed, for example, was inventory turns. But the vast majority of paper in the plant is customer owned, so we don't really have any control over the movement of that paper. It's been hard to sustain interest in the whole program when we see everyone else moving along and a lot of people being real enthusiastic about it. It's hard to sustain people's interest when they're not participants."

Then, too, games may create a conflict between short-term and long-term objectives. "We looked at doing an efficiency game," says Dick Anderson, a supervisor in the bindery. "If we could get a 5 percent gain over our budget numbers for this year—and a 5 percent gain is high—I think the payout would have come to $45 or $50. But people might have to give up some overtime, so they could actually wind up making less money. We have to find some way to align the incentives, or else the game won't work."

Scoreboards And Huddling

"Looking back," muses accounting supervisor John Smit, "I think our biggest challenge was to create the scoreboard. We spent six months. We got input from lots of folks all over the division on what a scoreboard ought to look like. The ideas were all over the place! But we eventually came up with a scoreboard that people agreed on."

Donnelley's scoreboard—one for each business unit within the division—is a two-page form. Page one is a modified income statement with about 20 lines, running the usual gamut from net sales to gross profit to earnings from operations to net operating profit after tax. At the bottom, a capital charge is deducted from net operating profit, leaving economic value added (EVA). The scoreboard team wanted to wind up with an EVA figure, because the corporation as a whole had decided to focus on boosting EVA.

Page two is a modified balance sheet that shows the capital-charge calculation that produces EVA. It adds cash and receivables, inventories, other capital, and net fixed assets to get a total net assets figure. It deducts liabilities and balance-sheet adjustments to get net capital employed. The EVA charge for any given month is simply net capital employed times the after-tax cost of capital (a percentage set by the corporation), with the result divided by 12.

But Donnelley's scoreboard is not simply a summary financial statement that could be prepared by any corporation's accountants. When you look next to each line item, for instance, there's a name. Smit:

> That individual is responsible for either preparing the number or seeing that it is prepared elsewhere in the organization. Then the person brings the number to the huddle and presents it. Alan Roufa fills in the spreadsheet at the meeting. It

shows up on an overhead, so we can see the income statement and balance sheet filled in as we go.

Next to the items, moreover, there are four columns: "budget," "forecast 1," "forecast 2," and "variance." Donnelley's huddles typically take place in the middle of a month. There, the attendees will offer opinions as to how the current month will end up, along with a preliminary estimate of the following month. So each month is subject to two forecasts, done a month apart. If the forecast is significantly different from the plant's budget, people responsible for the numbers are asked to explain. After the huddle, the scoreboard is put on E-mail; any interested employee can take a look at it to see where things stand.

Huddling, again, is one of the most challenging aspects of open-book management. Corporations rarely work that way. People aren't used to it. At Donnelley, forecasting was traditionally done by the controller. There were no broad-based meetings to review financials. Every department managed its own financial reports, and about ten senior managers would get together to review them. "That meeting looked at the past," says Smit. "What already happened. The huddle is looking to the future, what we think is going to happen."

So how well was Donnelley doing at huddling? Asked that question, the division's managers had mixed reactions. They were disappointed by the quality of the forecasts. ("Spotty," says Smit.) They felt they still had to involve more people in the company in producing the numbers that were reflected in the business unit's line items.

To an outside observer, though, they had made huge strides. Consider what the scoreboard-and-huddling process had already accomplished:

- People throughout the plant were seeing the same numbers and gradually learning what they meant. Several dozen people—including some hourly employees—were attending the huddles.

- Individual employees in some departments had taken on responsibility for producing their department's numbers for the month. Some employees had taken over specific line items, according to Tom Purcell, who manages one of the plant's business modules.

- Departments had developed scoreboards of their own and were trying to see that their numbers came out right. People working in the offset module, for example, were meeting to plan their upcoming work—and to discuss possible cost factors, such as overtime, that would affect their unit's performance.

Maybe most important, the process was forcing Donnelley to get better numbers. Accounting assumptions and procedures were being scrutinized. People were beginning to drill down to produce ever-more-detailed information. Alan Roufa, for instance—administrative manager for the East Plant—was working on a method for employees to track and forecast costs for each piece of equipment in their department. "Say there are nine presses in a department. You'd like each press to come up with its own income statement, or at least the expense side of the statement. Down the road, I think that's how we'll have to build the budget."

Still, Roufa was encouraged by what had happened so far. "Right now we tend to look at the department as a whole. We have a sense of how much work we're going to do in the next few months, and we have a sense of what our historical costs have been. And we sit down and say, 'Okay, what might be different from the historical view that we have of things? Am I involved in a project where the spending is now going to hit and that's not reflected in the budget? Do we have a lot of overtime coming?' Maybe we know we're going to be busy, so the historical number isn't going to be right.

"Trying to figure out those kinds of things, people are beginning to get a handle on how it all works. How it all fits together."

Geoff Benes concludes, "I think what we're learning is the process. The size of our organization makes processes like this take an awfully long time! But it's providing people with an education. We're building in trust, integrity, openness. And the more they get exposed to that, the more comfortable they will be."

Bonus-Plan Design

In November 1996, Robb convened yet another implementation team to discuss the bonus system. "It was a group of us representing all departments—managers, supervisors, and so forth. We started talking about what we wanted to accomplish, then came up with principles and assumptions about how we wanted it to unfold."

Before long, this original group had divided itself into several task teams:

> *Drivers* teams were charged with figuring out the key variables that drove business performance in each business unit. "There were four of them, because we have four business units in this division. Their role was to respond to a statement that went something like this: 'A successful 1997 depends on improving our performance in these key areas of the business.' In other words, what are the drivers of our businesses? We wanted to focus on no less than two and no more than five."

> A *mechanics* team had the job of coming up with methodologies. "Given these drivers, given how we will measure and track them, how will we come up with a payout bucket? The mechanics team worked with the drivers teams to establish performance thresholds and the methodology by which good performance would contribute to a payout bucket and poor performance would take from the bucket."

> An *administration* team was charged with figuring out administrative details. The plan had to be in compliance with applicable labor law. Eligibility rules needed to be established. The division would need policies for payments to employees (in accounting, for example) who served more than one business unit.

> Finally, a *communications* team was charged with implementing the plan. "Really, their job was twofold. First, it was to create the presentation and script to announce the plan. But second, they got all the managers and supervisors together to discuss integrating it with the rest of open-book management. How are we going to communicate the plan? What are we going to do with our scoreboards and our huddles? This performance-reward plan is now a piece that we can use to position our small games better, to make our huddles more meaningful, and so on."

The plan the teams began implementing in 1997 established both drivers and standards, or thresholds. In the East Plant print-and-bind operation, for example—one of the division's four business units—one driver was materials yield (essentially, how much paper is required to produce a given job). "We have a pretty aggressive budget number for materials yield," Robb explains, "and we have to bridge the gap between historical performance—what we've done in the past—and that budget number." He continues:

> So we might establish thresholds for each quarter, say, 2 percent improvement over historical performance the first quarter, 2.5 percent the second quarter, and so on.
>
> Then we'd look at it on a job-by-job basis. Those jobs that use less paper than the threshold would contribute savings to the bucket. Those that use more would pull money out of the bucket. Each of these drivers is measured in *dollars*. In this case, it's pounds of paper saved times price per pound. Better-than-threshold performance contributes to the bucket dollar for dollar, and worse-than-threshold performance detracts from the bucket dollar for dollar.
>
> At the end of the quarter we'll pay out a certain amount of the bucket: 5 to 15 percent the end of the first quarter, all the way up to 20 to 30 percent at the end of the fourth quarter. What determines how much we pay out *within* each quarter's range is our EVA number. The company has helped us establish some targets for EVA. If we just hit the target, the payout will be in the middle of the range. If we do slightly worse or slightly better, the payout will be adjusted accordingly.
>
> It's always going to be a cumulative number. At the end of any quarter, for example, you take the total cumulative amount in any bucket. Then you look at year-to-date EVA, which will determine the percentage of the bucket due to be shared, and you subtract any prior payments to get that quarter's payout. The advantage of this approach is that you could have mediocre performance during the year and still get a payout at the end of the year with a great fourth quarter. It keeps people in the game, like at SRC.

Donnelley wanted to distribute its bonus bucket equally among all employees, but U.S. labor law makes this procedure cumbersome for large companies. (Every person's hourly earnings must be recalculated to include the bonus, and that recalculation, in turn, establishes a new overtime rate for that individual.) Instead, it will distribute the bucket as a certain percentage of everybody's W-2 earnings.

Donnelley's companywide policies put a relatively low cap on the payout; it couldn't be more than 2 percent of total earnings.

(Employees are eligible for another 2 percent based on company-wide performance.) Robb and others believed that 2 percent wasn't a sufficient incentive. Still, they found that research into variable-compensation plans didn't necessarily support their concerns. In particular, an American Compensation Association study led by Jerry McAdams investigated 663 variable-pay plans and found that the most successful weren't necessarily those with the highest payouts; they were the plans with the most ongoing communication. "His conclusion," says Robb, "was that employees who feel valued, feel they have a say, can see how they impact the business—these employees need less financial reward than those who are less involved.

"When people expressed concerns about working within the corporate guidelines, I'd emphasize this. The 2 percent isn't much. But I said it isn't the amount of money, it's how we use the plan. If we communicate the way we should, if we use our scoreboards and our huddles, if we're teaching people and coaching people and doing the things we should be doing, well, the money will be nice. But the real lift will come from helping people to understand that they have a real role to play in this company's success."

Taking It to Another Business Unit

Donnelley began open-book management in the East Plant, which houses two of the division's four business units (known as modules at Donnelley). About a year after the launch, I spoke with a group of supervisors in the directory module at the West Plant—and got a capsule summary of how one group in a company can learn from another, build on what has already happened, yet implement open-book management on its own timetable. Here is how Scott Files, a supervisor in the module, described the process at that time.

> We started out last spring, around April and May, trying to understand what open-book management was all about. Most of us spent a couple of days at SRC to see it in action out there. And we spent some time hanging on the coattails of the East Plant! They were a little further along playing some games and so forth. We learned a lot from them as well. We continue to work with them.
>
> About six weeks ago, Don presented the East Plant business case for open-book management to the directory module. It

was why we're headed in that direction, what are the advantages of open-book management. That was presented to us [managers and supervisors] as a team. At that meeting we identified who was going to participate in the different teams: the focus-group team, the huddling team, the business-literacy-training teams. So we split up into different groups and sort of divided out assignments that way.

We also identified a sponsor team. Of course, John Bernard [manager of the module] is one of our sponsors. But we'll also have a controller on there, a building-operations person, people from different aspects of the business to help support this effort.

At that point the supervisors all went through a focus-group session, which Don facilitated. The same session that the hourly employees would go through. It was just to see where our heads were at and what we felt the business looked like. And whether we were prepared for open-book management.

Then, about three or four weeks ago, we put together the directory-module business case for open-book management. One thing we wanted to do as we took this to the workforce— we wanted to make sure there was a clear understanding of *why* we were doing this, what we hoped to gain from it, what was in it for them, what was in it for us. The goals and objectives. We took that business case and presented it to 50 employees across the module. Those employees were picked to go through the initial focus-group sessions.

So we did it in two groups. We presented the business case to the employees and gave them opportunities to ask questions. They were able to provide some input on some of their concerns, where they thought some of the roadblocks might be to open-book. That was some good input for us to receive. Then we split those 50 employees up into groups of 8 or 10 and sent them to the four-hour focus-group sessions.

Tomorrow, we're going to go over those results as a management team and talk about what we see there, what problems might come about as we go down this road. One thing we did commit to the hourly group of employees was that we're going to get them back together, reconvene, and present the results back to them. Make sure they feel comfortable with what they see on paper and start to develop some of that trust and respect that we know we need to work on between management and the workforce.

As for the next step, we have a team of what we're calling early adopters, which are hourly employees across the manufacturing areas. These are employees who we feel are interested in the business, who want to know where the money goes and how we can save a few bucks, who really want to get involved. We'll take them through the business case, so they understand it, and then start applying some of the business-literacy training to that group of early adopters. Right now it's 10 or 12 employees.

And then, overlapping some of the training efforts, will be some games. We'll identify some small games, just to get more people involved, even though they haven't been through any kind of formal training. We want to get them more involved in understanding the business and what role they play in saving a dollar here or there.

Not surprisingly, employees were raising a lot of questions about open-book management. Is this the program of the month? How can we do it when we're so busy? What's in it for me? ("They ask, 'Am I going to do this extra work, and you're going to be the only one who'll benefit?'" said Files.) The Donnelley managers and supervisors made a point of proceeding slowly. "With a lot of our other initiatives, we just threw it at them and said, 'This is what we're going to do,'" explains Neil Schwandt, another supervisor. "This time, we'll have a good foundation to build on. They can expect step one, step two, step three. And we're committed to all those steps." They also made a point of talking relentlessly about Donnelley's market situation and business needs. "At every crew meeting we talk about our competitive position," says John Bernard. "That sparks a little interest!"

Was Donnelley's venture into open-book management paying off? The East Plant, which was farthest along, had a very good year in 1996. Its experiment attracted the attention of other Donnelley units around the country. Yet managers such as manufacturing vice president Benes are appropriately cautious in attributing too much of the good performance to open-book management. It's not a quick fix, they point out. It takes time to affect people's thinking and behavior. The real test will be two, three, five years down the road.

On the other hand, when I spent time at the division, I could feel something new in the air; something that had employees and managers alike turned on, excited, optimistic about their own future and the company's. That something was open-book management, and it is hard to imagine that it did not play a sizable role in boosting the division's performance.

A Way of Thinking

This is a business book. It describes a new approach to running a company. But it isn't just about business; it's about how people can work together in ways that are both satisfying and productive.

There are a lot of specifics in this book: specifics about scoreboards, bonus plans, teaching tools, and so on. But what's important isn't the specifics, it's the ideas that underlie them, the way of thinking. After all, when you boil open-book management down to its basics, you get some pretty commonsensical notions about how people in almost any situation can do a better job.

The first of these ideas: People at work need some easily understandable measurements—scoreboards—and they need to know how those measurements fit into the big picture.

It's amazing how many of us go to work each day without really knowing what constitutes doing a good job. "Work" comes to mean serving whoever walks in the door, or responding to whatever the boss demands, or handling the paperwork that shows up on the desk. Are we effective? Is the organization we work for effective? Is it improving or getting worse? Who knows? Unless there are metrics—numbers—to watch, we don't have a clue.

The numbers don't have to be purely financial. Public-sector and nonprofit organizations, for example, have missions other than simply making money for shareholders. They are charged with carrying out policies, enforcing the law, serving the needy, delivering services such as education or medical care. They need one set of measurements that lets them know how well they are performing their mission. They need a separate set—budget and financial numbers—to tell them whether they're performing it in a cost-effective manner.

To be sure, plenty of organizations do a lot of counting. They count calls handled, number of hours billed, number of parts produced per hour, number of clients seen or claims processed, and so on. Trouble is, all these measurements are imposed and enforced by management, without any visible connection to anything that matters. Employees learn how to game these systems. They make sure somebody else gets the time-consuming jobs. They pursue the goals that get measured and forget about other goals, such as quality and good service. They fudge the figures, often with the support of their immediate bosses, who understand that making the numbers isn't always the only objective worth pursuing.

Open-book management brings two extra dimensions to measurement. (1) It ties specific numbers—the numbers by which people gauge their performance—to the big picture. People learn the connection between what they do every day and the success of their organization. That gives the numbers a meaning they don't otherwise have. (2) Open-book managers don't hand the numbers down from on high. The creation of metrics is a two-way street. It starts not with a managerial dictum, but with questions. How will we in this department know if we are doing a better job? How will we know if we are contributing to the success of the organization? Organizations need to know how they measure success. The people who work for them need to know those measurements and to understand how they contribute to that success. Until they do, they'll just keep on doing whatever's put in front of them.

The second major idea is: People need goals—and should have a hand in setting them.

Without goals, measurements don't mean much. With goals, the numbers take on a new importance. They show how you're doing in relation to your objective. They let you know whether you're winning or losing.

The big-picture goals of a business are easy to understand. A company wants to increase shareholder value. It wants to increase profits. These long-term objectives dictate shorter-term ones (gain market share, introduce new products). Big-picture objectives can be broken down into their component parts (reduce scrap, improve customer service, make this particular store profitable).

It isn't so different in nonbusiness contexts, though the objectives may be less easily measurable. A nonprofit medical clinic wants to provide excellent health care to its client population within the parameters set by its budget. A school wants to serve the educational needs of its students, within reasonable spending constraints. These goals may not be perfectly quantifiable, but they are certainly able to be assessed. How does the client population feel about the service they're getting? How do the professionals involved—doctors, teachers, and so on—feel about the service they're delivering? Where are the strengths and the weaknesses? What are the goals for improvement?

As with numbers, goals handed down from above aren't too inspiring. Goals created from below because people understand the big picture and want to help the organization improve are much more so. They also tend to be more ambitious than any set of goals managers would dare devise. Open-book management assumes that people know the goals they're shooting for. It also assumes they should have a hand in setting those goals.

The third idea is: In the right framework, people will hold each other accountable—and will work better because of it.

In conventional organizations, managers are accountable for seeing that the work gets done. That's their job. They supervise, instruct, ask, threaten, cajole, persuade, and otherwise motivate employees to do what they want done. In open-book organizations, people hold themselves accountable. They see and understand the metrics that gauge their performance, help establish their own goals, and worry (together) about how to solve problems that get in their way.

So does the manager's job disappear? Only if you believe that all the people in an organization already know all they need to know—and that they're always well-meaning, cooperative, astute in their judgments, and skilled at interpersonal communication. A manager in an open-book organization has a whole lot to do, as coach and teacher and facilitator. What he or she doesn't have to do is make employees do the work.

The fourth idea is: People need to feel that they're fairly treated—in other words, that it's all worth it.

Some critics of open-book management deride its reliance on bonuses and financial incentives as somehow demeaning and instead urge that employees learn to take satisfaction in a job well done or a customer well served. This objection misses the point that the whole idea of a business is to make money—and if people at the top are getting rich while you and I are making no more than our regular hourly wage, it's going to be tough for us to get too excited about doing that job well.

But bonus or variable-compensation systems aren't like the food pellets dispensed to laboratory pigeons. They're rarely enough to motivate people by themselves. Their importance lies in the human messages they send: We're all in this together. We'll all share in the fruits of our efforts. Without a message of this sort, people are likely to feel exploited, that they're being asked to work harder for somebody else's benefit.

This view of financial incentives sheds some light on applying open-book management outside the business context. It really doesn't matter, for example, that a nonprofit can't pay a big bonus, or that a public agency can't pay a bonus at all. What matters is that the success of the organization in reaching its goals be shared. That message can be communicated in a hundred different ways: awards and thank-yous, token rewards such as gift certificates, parties and celebrations, more-generous time-off policies, and so on. If people feel that they've contributed to a real accomplishment and that their contribution is recognized rather than slighted, that may be reward enough.

There's one final idea lurking here as well, and this may be the most fundamental way in which open-book thinking about organizations and work differs from conventional thinking.

For a century—maybe more—an adversarial attitude has permeated U.S. business culture. The people inside an organization are "us." The people outside are "them." Companies have been secretive, even hostile, not only toward their competitors, but also toward their suppliers, customers, and clients. Within the organization, there are other kinds of us-versus-thems: management versus labor, home-office staff versus people in the field, our craft or profession or department versus yours, and so on. Companies are collections of competing classes and fiefdoms, riven with mistrust and shot through with internal politics.

Nothing this side of Judgment Day is going to make the adversarial attitude vanish completely. But open-book management works on the assumption that people within organizations (and even in different organizations) have common interests as well as potentially conflicting ones. If they can set out common objectives, with measurements that everybody understands and a system of joint accountability in which everyone participates, they can emphasize those common interests—and the result will be both more productive and more satisfying. Here are some examples:

Dealing with suppliers. The old way of working with suppliers and vendors was: Keep them at arm's length; beat them down on price; hold your own cards close to the vest. Today, that's changing. Companies like to think they're creating partnerships with suppliers. So why not sit down together, come up with common goals and measurements, then brainstorm how to accomplish them? One of Amoco Canada's facilities, for example, uses contract labor— and invites the labor supplier to sit in on its regular financial meetings and estimate upcoming costs. That regular meeting, say Amoco managers, has led to productive discussions about how both sides can save money.

Annual raises. Companies these days are hard-pressed to give regular annual raises. But employees still expect them and sometimes threaten unionization or strikes if they're not given. This is a traditionally adversarial situation, but it doesn't need to be. If people work together to boost performance—and share a healthy portion of the profits that derive from that better performance— everybody wins. Southwest Airlines and its pilots' union understood this principle when they negotiated a ten-year deal that gave the pilots no raise for five years but more stock ownership. Southwest kept its costs under control, and the pilots stood to share in the increased value produced by cost control. (Meanwhile, American and other airlines were bogged down in traditional you-can-afford-it–no-we-can't wage negotiations with their pilots.)

The Is-this-just-a-business? complaint. You've heard the gripe from any number of sources. Nonprofit and public-sector employees complain about budget constraints. Even in businesses, creative types such as designers and engineers resent the bottom line. And all these people are right—up to a point. What they do isn't necessarily governed by monetary concerns. You can't always capture the value of a piece of research or a clever new design—let alone the work of a nonprofit or public agency—on a financial statement. But though many organizations aren't *just* businesses, every organization is a business in one sense: it doesn't have unlimited resources and so must accomplish its ends in a cost-effective manner. Open-book management teaches people to understand and manage this constraint, precisely so that they can accomplish whatever else is important to them.

"We teach our people," says the manager of a sophisticated video-production studio, "you get to be an artist so long as this—the income statement—tells a positive story. If it doesn't, you don't get to be an artist any more."

Budgets. Large organizations work like government agencies (or the former Soviet Union). Department heads fight for budget allocations, which are determined from above. Then they do their best to spend as much as they possibly can, so they'll be justified in asking for more next year. Power and status are determined by the size of your budget.

Budgets are inevitable in any large organization; resources have to be allocated somehow, and budgets are a useful tool. What's not inevitable is the idea that people should be rewarded for overspending their budgets. Open-book companies expect managers and employees to figure out ways to save money in their annual budgets while accomplishing the same objectives, because that contributes to business performance.

Layoffs. No matter what, some people will lose jobs through no fault of their own. That's the way a free-enterprise system works, and it isn't likely to change. On the other hand, the wholesale downsizings of recent years amount to nothing less than a massive failure of managerial imagination. The same people who allowed companies to get fat and bloated are somehow unable to do anything with the people on their payroll other than give them pink slips.

But suppose a company does boost its performance to the point at which some of its people are no longer needed? Can't those same skills be applied to the creation of new products, new services, new business niches? That's essentially what Springfield ReManufacturing Corporation has done. The company that was one struggling business unit a decade and a half ago now has more than 12 units, most of them profitable. Every business unit provides an entrepreneurial opportunity for managers—and many, many jobs for employees.

This list could go on, but maybe it—and the book—should come to a close. I hope you've learned a new way of thinking here, along with plenty of useful tools and techniques for applying it in your business. As you do, we'll all learn more about this evolving theory of working together. Open-book management is an ongoing tale—and the next chapters have yet to be written.

Resources

For a free list of resources relating to open-book management—books, a newsletter, videos, software, training programs, and so on—send your request to the author at 37A Prentiss Street, Cambridge, Massachusetts 02140 USA; fax: (617)492-3607; E-mail: jcase@hbsp.harvard.edu. Or you may visit the World Wide Web site: www.openbookmanagement.com.

Acknowledgments

I owe special thanks for this book to my friend and colleague Karen Carney, managing editor of *Open-Book Management: Bulletin*. Karen not only gathered up much of the information contained in the book, she also kept the business going while the ostensible editor-and-publisher was worrying more about his prose than about his product. I'm not quite sure how she manages it all. I am sure that I'm very, very grateful.

I also owe special thanks to Vera Gibbons. Vera spent countless hours talking to people from open-book companies, and in the process proved herself a skilled and savvy interviewer. She, too, contributed much of the information contained in this book.

As always, the folks in and around Springfield ReManufacturing Corporation and The Great Game of Business were an indispensable source of help and support. I have learned more from Jack Stack than from any other ten people I can think of. Jay Burchfield, David Lough, Bill Fotsch, Dave LaHay, and their associates were extraordinarily generous with their time, their ideas, and their network of contacts. So was my longtime friend and colleague Bo Burlingham.

Finally, I'd like to thank the many, many men and women who are building open-book companies and who took the time to share their experiences. I wish the list that follows were complete, but I know it is not. Some companies requested anonymity, both for themselves and for their employees. At other companies, I spoke with so many people that I have given up hope of listing every name. To those I have omitted, my apologies. To them and to everyone listed below, my heartfelt gratitude.

Eric DeLong of Acorn Manufacturing Co.; Michael Kudryk of ACuPowder International; Dennis Bakke of AES Corp.; Dan Rothaupt and the lunch group at AES Thames; David Short of Amherst Woodworking & Supply; Bob Taylor, Fred Plummer, Stacey Norman, and several other people at Amoco Canada; Dan Kaplan and Danny Warshay of Anchor Communications; Randy Stockton of Arning Industries; Paul Centenari of Atlas Container; Jennifer Pearl of Bagel Works; Fred Saul of Bay State Press; Jim Annis and Timothy Shields of Bonanza Nut & Bolt; Shirley Heusel of Boston Laser Plus; Steven Green of Boundless Technologies; Doreen Eng of Braas Co.; John Schuster and Jill Carpenter of Capital Connections; John DeMaine of Carolina Safety Associates; Bill Friedman of Cascade Bookkeeping; Carolyn Chandler of Chandler Properties; Joe Clark and Jim Brown of Chick-fil-A; Suzanne Kreitzberg of SBK Human Resources Consulting, who is affiliated with Colburn-Bertholon-Rowland; Don Scarlata of Colonial Mills; Pat Ekdahl of Columbia Regional Medical Center Southwest Florida; Bill Palmer and a whole lot of other people at Commercial Casework; Larry Cone of Cone Software; Gary Jackson of Cornwell, Jackson Group; Michael Crisp and Brent Youngblood of Crisp Publications; the Critzes and their friends at Critz Inc.; Bill LaPrade and his associates at Digital Semiconductor; Gerard Danos of Dixie Iron Works; Dan Schweitzer of Docu-Net; Lynn Topic of Dolphin Quest; Don Robb, Geoff Benes, John Bernard, John Hallgren, Buddy Ganse, Jim Burrows, and many other people at RR Donnelley & Sons; Ed Zimmer and George Forbes of ECCO; Steve Sheppard, Chuck Mayhew and Doug Westra of Foldcraft; Julie Lotesto of Glavin Security Specialists; Alan Lewis, Martha Prybylo, and Priscilla O'Reilly of Grand Circle Corp.; Jim Meyerdirk of GT Development; Gloria Hale of Hale Glass, Inc.; Mary Jo Burt and Mike Rydin of HCSS; Ron Stewart of Heflin Steel; Bill Renick and Jim Siegel of Hexacomb Corp.; Rick Haarstad of Hydraulic Specialty Co.; Steve Carr of IPT Corp.; Dale Hoffmann of Jim's Formal Wear; Mark Smith and Leslie Fishbein of Kacey Fine Furniture; Chris LaBarge of LaBarge Products; Ken McBride of Lawyers Title of Oklahoma City; Frank Topinka of McKenna Professional Imaging; Holly Smith-Bove of Motherwear; Richard Weiss and Jim Ahern of Mountain Travel Sobek; Tom Neilsen of Neilsen Manufacturing; Bruce Nims of Nims Associates; Michael Taylor of OASIS Inc.; David Robbins of Omega Point Labs; Judy Hurley of PARCA; Kim Kenyon of Pettit Fine Furniture; Patrick Kelly of Physician Sales & Service; Bill Pickens of Pool Covers; Andy Powell-Williams; Peggy Wynne Borgman of Preston Wynne; Kim Ferguson and Shawna Gygi of PTI; John Cappelletti of Putman Publishing; Larry Friedman of Reimbursement Services; Don Miller and Ted Castle of Rhino Foods; Tina Comstock of RTW Minnesota; Mark Stewart of Schrock Cabinet Co.; Edie Heilman and Sue Meehan of Share Group; Jeff

Swogger of Sharpsville Quality Products; Samuel Smith of Smith & Co. Engineers; Dirk Macfarlane of Sony Display Device; Randy Johnson of S&R Industries; Joyce Douglas and Karen Berman of Syncor International; Phil Hindmarch of Ten Thousand Waves; Harden Blackwell of Terminix of North Carolina; Lynn Thompson of Thompson Pontiac GMC Cadillac; Deborah Field of Transitions for Health; Kevin Ruble of TranSolutions; Mimi Taylor of Vectra; Chad Engler of Visual In-Seitz; Joan Beisel and many other people at Wascana Energy; Hugh McGill, Charles Edmundsen, Calvin Arey, and Rob Zicaro of Web Converting; Larry Krieger of The WellBridge Company; Steve Wilson, formerly of Mid-States Technical; Terry Fulwiler of Wisconsin Label; Sarah Montgomery of Woodpro Cabinetry.

Also: Alicia Stark of Air Experts; Carla Argetsinger of Anheuser-Busch; Peter Sector of BAS Inc.; Richard Vogt of Biotechtronix; Susan Gifford of BRPH Architects-Engineers; Michael Bryant of Career Transition Services; Dale Fraaza of Cargo Heavy Duty; Randy Fulmer of Carolina Equipment and Supply; Richard Harshaw of Carrier Corp.; Cynthia Driscoll Graham of CDG & Associates; Bill Efird of Coastal Air Conditioning; Townes Duncan, then with Comptronix; Mark Clark of Courtesy Aircraft; Ralph Hilsman, Creative Edge; Beth Schoelkopf of Dun & Bradstreet; George Adams Jr. of Electric Supply of Tampa; Becky Cannon of Family Clubhouse; Peter Visceglia of Federal Business Centers; Linda Francis; David Gasper of Gasper Corp.; Tim Timoteo of R.J. Gator's; Ken Bricker of Gen Corp.; Peter Novak of General Parts; David Hawk of Gertrude Hawk Chocolates; Randy Gilliland of G&R Metals; Jim Boone of Hartman Management; Dan Chiles of Heatway; Jim Taylor of Hometown Distributing; Carlos Rivera of Hudson Eagle Distributing Co.; Shawn Connors of International Health Awareness Center; Howard Fullerton and Frank Hovey of Inventronics; Jim Gilpin of Iola Bank & Trust Co.; Craig Perkins of Islands of Success; Janice Kay, formerly with Kinko's; Gary Crose of Landmark; Randy Dipner of Meeting the Challenge; Brad Meyer, formerly with Memorex Telex; Michael Caslin of the National Foundation for Teaching Entrepreneurship; Don Long of New Holland Custom Woodworking; Gregory Rice of New World Technologies; Maria Paine; Richard Tenney of Page One Healthcare Solutions; Charm Alexander-McPhee of P.K.G. Industries; Hank Epstein of The Quality Coach; Mary Baechler of Racing Strollers; Keith Lowe of Rheyn Technologies; Sam Sanchez and Ron Williamson of RJW Inc.; Deb

Kessler of Room & Board; Tom Kunz of Shell Western E&P; Chris Meeker of SIGNS of the Times; John Lorentzen of St. Charles Lumber; Scott Dohner of Superfleet Inshoe Systems; Bruce Kelling and his associates at Tiburon; Chip Flynn of Transport Management Group; Curtis Hamilton at TRI-AD Actuaries; Cathy Petersen of Vacations Inc.; John D. Wayne of Vandor Corp.; Walter Henritze III of Wave Inc.; and John VanDeusen of Work Systems Associates.

I would also like to thank Chuck Kremer, of Educational Discoveries, Inc., and Corey Rosen, of the National Center for Employee Ownership. I have learned much from both.

My wife, Quaker Case, offered all kinds of help and support for this book—even though living with a writer is sometimes no picnic.

INDEX

Made in the USA
Lexington, KY
21 April 2011